CONTEMPLATIVE PRAYER

Problems and an Approach
for the Ordinary Christian

Rev. Alan J. Placa

LIVING FLAME PRESS
BOX 74 LOCUST VALLEY, N.Y. 11560

All quotations of scripture are from the *New American Bible*.

Cover: Robert Manning

Nihil Obstat: Rev. George A. Denzer, D.D., S.T.D.·*Censor Librorum*, July 17, 1976.

Imprimatur: Most Rev. John R. McGann, D.D., Bishop of Rockville Centre, July 22, 1976.

Published by: Living Flame Press / Locust Valley / New York 11560

Copyright 1976: Alan J. Placa

ISBN: 0-914544-13-6

Printed in the United States of America

To
The Most Reverend Walter P. Kellenberg, D.D.
First Bishop of Rockville Centre:

Through his ministry
and by the imposition of his hands
I became a priest of Jesus Christ.

Contents

Preface

This small book is the summary of a series of talks which I have given several times over the past few years to various groups of people. Regardless of the nature of the group, the question they posed was always the same: they asked for direction in prayer.

There are many "first questions" which draw people to examine Christian faith more deeply. Some are concerned for morality: they wish to become better persons, and to be more open and compassionate toward their fellowmen. Some feel "at sea" in a modern world which seems to have no absolute values, and wish to rediscover the gospel as a source of direction and an anchor for their lives. Some are attracted by Christ's social message and by the Church's centuries-old commitment to ease the burdens of the suffering. Some young people, disillusioned by the hollowness of contemporary society, are intrigued by the transcendent and mystical aspects of Christianity. Others are moved by Christ's simple message of love and peace in a family of brothers and sisters.

Whatever the "first questions" may have been that drew a specific group together, by the time they had invited me to speak to them they had reached a point which all Christians must eventually reach: the point where the essential question is not how to do this or that, or how to act in this way or that way, but rather, how to come into more realistic and prayerful contact with the Lord.

In the last analysis, there is only one thing about myself that can determine the effectiveness and the authenticity of my living the Christian gospel. That one thing is to be found in the answer to this question: "Can men see Jesus Christ through me?" In other words, a believing and witnessing Christian must be a person who is transparent enough for others to be able to look through him and through his words and actions and see the Lord Jesus living and operating in his life.

Usually, the human spirit has a certain opacity to it: as we grow older we build up more and more defenses against the world outside of ourselves, and the image we present to men is usually the opaque image of those many defenses. It is precisely through prayer that the clarity and transparency of Christian living and witness come to the soul.

If I am not a prayerful person, then men cannot see Jesus Christ through me. They will see only my own quirks and defenses, only the complex of de-

8

vices I have put together to protect myself from others, from myself, and from God. I will have deceived no one but myself, and men will see that I am a fraud. They will certainly come to suspect my motivation for speaking in an apparently religious way, and they may also come to suspect the entire religious enterprise.

I may have many specific things to say to a group of Catholic people about the details of ministry within the Church, or about theology or the sacraments or the teachings of the Church; but I am afraid to say those things to any group before I come to know them. I am afraid that I may mislead them into believing that my observations about the details of Christian living or about ministry as a science and a craft are sufficient: they are not.

We have the Lord's word for it: there are very few things really necessary to the true life of the Christian, " . . . you worry and fret about so many things, and yet few are needed, indeed only one. It is Mary who has chosen the better part; it is not to be taken from her" (*Luke 10:41-42*). It is that "better part," the life of contemplative prayer as it can be realized by ordinary Christians in the world, which we will examine in these pages.

Part One:
Growth In Prayer

Relationship With The Lord

If we believe that prayer is our means of communicating with God, then we must have some understanding of the nature of our relationship with Him before we can speak meaningfully about prayer as communication. To say that we want to understand how we are related to God is to raise one of the most fundamental of all religious problems: how can we know anything about God Who is the "Unknown"? I am not speaking about the kind of fundamental knowledge about God that we can get from His self-gift of revelation, I am speaking about personal knowledge of His action and power and presence in our own lives. How can we ever know that in our experiences we are contacting Him and not our own imaginations?

There is a very basic principle which applies to

all the sciences, including theology, which we must borrow here. The correct procedure in any investigation whose purpose is to expand the horizon of our knowledge is to move from the known to the unknown. Children studying algebra for the first time are bewildered and frustrated when they face a simple equation like $2 + x = 6$. Their frustration comes from the fact that they move immediately to the *unknown* and ask, "What is x?" When they learn the correct methodology, their frustration will dissipate because they will learn to approach the problem more reasonably by first searching for all the meaning they can find in the terms they *already know*. When they examine what they already know about the other terms, about 2 and 6, they can solve the problem because they understand the relationship between the known quantities and can then deduce that the unknown quantity must be 4.

There is much frustration in religious living for those who want to go immediately to the most profound religious questions, skipping over the simpler things we already know — by God's grace — about ourselves and the world we live in. If a man wishes to understand the nature of his relationship with God and insists on asking simply, "What is my relationship to God?" or, "Who is God?" — then that man faces unavoidable bewilderment: no man can presume to pretend he knows Who God is, and no man can pretend that he understands man's relationship to God. Instead, men must search for as much meaning as they can find in the terms they already know: men must try to understand the nature of relationships with

14

which they are already familiar before pretending they can leap to an appreciation of the more profound relationship of God and man.

Our human relationships are of two fundamental kinds, they are either primarily *functional* or primarily *personal*. If we could think of such a thing, a *purely functional* relationship would be one within which the identities of the individuals involved made no difference at all. But such a situation is nearly inconceivable, and one would have to be a monster to maintain *purely* functional relationships. Although my relationship to the butcher, for example, is primarily functional, I do have some degree of personal concern for him: if he were taken ill while filling my order I simply couldn't step over him in search of another butcher to serve my needs. I would have at least enough personal interest to see to *his* personal needs at the moment. The same qualification must be offered for personal relationships. A personal relationship is one in which the matter of greatest importance is the identity and presence of the other person: it really doesn't matter how two people function together if they are in love because they derive deep satisfaction from each other's presence. In many friendships I experience mild panic when I "run out of things to say" and when we cannot think of interesting things to do. This can never happen in a real loving relationship because that relationship is built on the inherent sufficiency of the presence of the other for my happiness. When I truly love another human being we may sit in a room for hours without ever saying a word, and yet be completely at ease and, what is more, be able to say honestly that the time was well spent and enjoyable because we were sharing each other's presence. Perhaps the heart of the matter is even clearer when we begin not from the point of presence but from the point of absence: if a person I love deeply is absent from me, then no amount of interesting distraction will bring me real and personal satisfaction until I am once again in the presence of my beloved.

But, just as one would have to be a monster in order to sustain a *purely* functional relationship, so one would have to have significant personal deficiencies in order to sustain a *purely personal* relationship. Just as good human balance demands that there be some degree of personalism in primarily functional relationships, so the same balance requires that those who are personally committed to one another in love engage in functional activities. A purely personal love which never expressed itself in words and actions and shared experiences would be arid and adolescent: it would be a "secret" love never expressed and never acted out.

One of the things that distinguishes real love from mere acquaintance is that love is deeply creative. I am always attracted to another when it is apparent to me that we have certain mutual needs and resources: that the other person has certain needs and that I have personal resources for the fulfilling of those needs, and that I have needs and the other possesses resources for filling my needs. I may be attracted to another person because of a mutual interest in art, or sports, or literature, or science, or even religion. But so long as our relationship remains at the level of fulfilling already recognized personal needs it remains acquaintance and not love. Love drives me to discover new needs and resources in myself. When I love another person I come to observe that the other has needs which I do not believe I can fulfill, but my love drives me to discover deep within myself personal resources I did not know I possessed. When I love another person I come to observe that the other has resources which I do not believe I need, but my love drives me to discover deep within myself personal needs I did not know existed.

All of the foregoing is said about human interpersonal relationships: it is said in reference to the nature of relationships as we already know them in the world. To understand our relationship with the Lord we must be able to move from the known to the unknown: from what we already know about the relationships, in which human persons engage, to this new and more profound level of relationship between the human person and the divine Persons: Father, Son, and Holy Spirit.

Only the most immature of children have purely functional relationships with God: they are aware of His existence only in their own need, and they turn to Him only to satisfy that need. On the other hand, a purely personal relationship with God would also be quite immature, but in a peculiarly "adult" way. There are many people who claim to have deeply "personal" relationships with the Lord, and yet they claim that there is no need for them to express that relationship in religious activity, especially in membership in a church, because they know the Lord so deeply "within themselves." I refer to this particular immaturity as peculiarly "adult" because it is made of the same presumption that has killed so many human relationships: when one person presumes that he knows another so well that it is not necessary to speak, to explain, to offer and seek affection, to risk humiliation and rejection, to engage in the many functions that prove and feed love, then that person has already destroyed his relationship with the other; he has destroyed it by reducing the other to a thing so small that it can fit into his head.

Our relationship with God must have both personal and functional dimensions, it must be a creative relationship of true love. It does, naturally, begin by a recognition of mutual "needs" and "resources," but it must move beyond that fundamental stage. Of course a believing man must see that God offers things which are desirable: salvation, mercy, love, security, and so forth. And then too, a man recognizes that he is willing to give to God certain things which He demands: obedience, loyalty, purity, service, and so forth. But the breakthrough to love is made, for example, when I realize that God is offering me more than I thought, that He is offering me things I did not know I desired: a deeper life of prayer and a more profound compassion for my fellowmen. With the realization that He is offering me these new "resources" of His, I discover deep in myself new personal "needs," a new desire for these very things. Similarly, the love of God will make me feel other new needs in myself, and it will lead me to discover more of God's infinite power and personal resources.

It is within the context of this understanding of

our relationship with God that we must analyze our growth in prayer. Because prayer is the expression of a complex and creative relationship of love, it is a *struggle*. Because it implies achieving the correct balance of functionalism and personalism, and because it demands loving attention to the needs and resources of God and myself, it must be a *growing in familiarity*. And, finally, because prayer is the most intimate moment of our life lived in union with the Lord it must be a mutual *sharing* of ourselves with God and with other believers.

We will try to appreciate prayer from each of these points of view: as a struggle, as a growing in familiarity with the Lord, and as a sharing process. After this we will turn our attention to a style of prayer which may be helpful in growing in the life of the Lord.

A New Way Of Knowing

One thing that is necessary, if we are to speak in a meaningful way about growth in prayer, is that we must have some idea of the purpose or goal of our prayer life. I say our prayer *life* to distinguish the overall process by which we grow in our faith from the more "short-term" petitions that we make in moments of need. When we pray out of our immediate practical needs the purpose of praying is obvious. What we must get at here is not that obvious point, but rather the larger question of why it is important to develop a prayer life which is more or less independent of our immediate needs. Most of us have needs that are complex enough that we *could* very well spend every waking minute simply cataloguing our needs in fervent prayer and asking God to fulfill them all. But, if we return to the analogy of human interpersonal relations, we could spend all our time with people we love just "doing" things — there are so many things to be done — and then our relationships would gradually slip away from us, and the other person would become less and less real, in himself, and more and more a creature of our need to "do." We would stop caring for one another as unique individuals, each with our own special life and identity, and would begin to suck one another up into our own private worlds and projects.

The same would happen to our religious lives if we allowed ourselves free rein only to express our needs to God. Every kind of relationship into which we enter must be a carefully nurtured thing; we must be respectful of the other and we must be anxious to discover our deepest need: the need for the presence and love of the other. In other words, in our human relationships, we can honestly say that the one thing we need above all else from the one we love is *knowledge* of the beloved and a new knowledge of ourselves as we are seen through the eyes of those we love. These words have very practical implications for our human relationships. We can come to know one another *intellectually* in many ways. The simplest way is to begin to learn about the other person's past. To be familiar with the things that a man has suffered, and the things that have brought him joy, is to come to know him. There is another kind of "intellectual" knowledge of the other person that is rooted in our continuing observation of the other. I come to know what a person likes and dislikes, what he needs and what he abhors, and I grow in my ability to offer the things he needs and to ask for the things he needs to give. Then again, there is another way we come to know one another, an experiential one, where we begin to share each other's lives. Quite beyond whatever intellectual knowledge I may have of one whom I love, however subtle that knowledge may be, there is a way in which I come to "grasp" those I love in a manner that is far beyond the intellectual.

When a woman comes to me and describes a life of nearly pure horror with her husband, a life of beatings and insults, of faithlessness and abuse, she touches me very deeply and I reach out to her in compassion. But when she goes on to tell me that in spite of it all she still loves this man, she brings me face to face with a mystery. All logic and common sense dictate that she must leave this intolerable situation. Charity moves me to pity the woman and help her to extricate herself from her misery, but I am stopped short by one unpredictable piece of information — she claims she still feels love. The problem is that I am grasping the situation intellectually and logically, observing and evaluating all the data and the variables and drawing a sound conclusion. The reality of the matter is that the woman is "grasping" the situation by virtue of another power, a power beyond logic. She has experienced this man in a far richer complex of experiences; she has managed to see, beyond the visible and measurable, into the man's identity and within it she has seen something valuable and lovable. She has come to know him through experiences that I have not shared and cannot share.

But our religious living introduces a whole new

problem. Can we truly say that our goal is to *know* God? How could we know Him? Could there be any meaningful intellectual knowledge? Certainly there is the Scriptural "information" about God, and certainly there is a rich tradition of theological insight into His life and nature, but would all of that be satisfactory? Would it be any more satisfactory than the purely intellectual knowledge of a lover would be? That kind of knowledge is necessary but it is not sufficient; we do want and need more than that. In fact, in human relationships "intellectual" knowledge, however subtle, independent of the "experiential" kind of knowing, would not lead to love at all. My intellectual grasp of that woman's husband led me to hate him, but her experiential grasp of him led her to love him in spite of the "data." But where does all of that leave us? How can we have "experiential" knowledge of God? Or, to put it another way, how can we come to love God? In the ordinary scheme of things we come to love persons after we have known them; in other words, the "experiential" is based on the "intellectual" when we speak of love. We come to grasp a person deeply and to experience him as lovable only after we have been able to observe and understand him intellectually.

The problem in our relationship with God is that our intellectual knowledge of Him is "once removed," so to speak. It is not a direct knowledge of the person, but rather a knowledge of Him through the Scriptures, through other peoples' reflection upon the Scriptures, and through reflection on the world God has made. If love of God means anything, then, it must be rooted in a different kind of knowledge. The knowledge of God which leads to our love of Him is knowledge in faith, and our prayer lives are the active dimension of our lives of faith.

At this point you might justifiably be saying to yourself, "Well, why didn't he come out and say that at the outset?" It does seem that I've used quite a few words to say something that most religious people take for granted. And yet I don't judge our exercise, thus far, to be a waste of time. There is an ancient principle of method in theology that holds that good theology must begin with a simply stated doctrine, must undertake some more or less complicated digression from the simplicity of the statement, and finally return to the original statement. The purpose of the "excursion" is to return to the starting point with a fresh sense of its truth. It is often said that the most pleasant part of traveling is returning home, that one comes to appreciate the comfort and security of home more and more with each pleasant trip away from home. It's not that my home changes when I am away from it, rather I change and grow and come to know myself better and, in my return, bring more of myself to the task of appreciating what I have at home. So it is in religious reflection. If I can begin with a simple statement of doctrine or faith and then let myself reflect on it with new interest and new implications, with a new sense of my own situation in faith, then I will return to make exactly the same original statement, once again, and find in that original statement new depths of meaning *for me* because the excursion has revealed new dimensions of myself.

It is important that we come to understand faith in a more vibrant way so that we can undertake a renewed life of prayer. For far too many, the word "faith" is a way of ending conversations. "Faith" is considered a magic power through which the initiated are privy to special knowledge not available to the uninitiated. To be sure, faith is a mysterious thing but mystery should never be a conversation stopper; it should be the beginning of a lifelong conversation. When I described the hypothetical situation of the woman in love with her apparently cruel husband, I said that her revelation of her love for the man brought me into contact with mystery. I didn't mean that I would end my conversation with her by saying, "Well isn't that a hell of a thing! I guess your feelings for him are beyond me!" I meant that an encounter with something so mysterious should motivate me to achieve some further insight into the situation and into the woman's feelings. Now, in fact, if I were to commit myself to attaining real insight into the situation I might be undertaking an impossible task. Mysteries are only penetrated when we commit our lives to them. The mystery of her love for her husband has unfolded before the woman precisely because she has made the gift of her life to him. Most likely, I am not prepared to give my life to him in the same way.

Understanding faith requires the same life commitment. Many people, especially young people, are at a loss to understand where one would begin to live the life of faith. I am not sure I can give a good theoretical answer to that question, but I do know that I can tell the story of my beginnings in faith. I know that, at one time, I went through a systematic process of rejecting my Catholic faith. First I rejected the Sacrament of Penance, but held on to all the rest. Then I rejected the Real Presence of the Eucharist, but held on to all the rest. Then all the sacraments went, then Christ's divinity, and finally, my very faith in the existence of God disappeared. How easy it is to summarize those months of agony in a few lines. How many of the steps I've left out and how many I have already forgotten! But the process was relentless and it reached its conclusion. By the time I was eighteen years old I was a nonbeliever.

The return process was even more difficult, and even more complicated, but I can isolate one moment in which my return to faith was as inevitable as my fall from it had been. At one point, I became so consumed by the question of whether faith *could* mean anything to me again that I decided to do something which I thought was a bit shoddy and dishonest, at the time. I decided to *try* it; I decided to start living *as if* I believed and to test whether I felt and seemed authentic in the attempt. I wanted to know whether I would feel like a man of integrity and whether others would see me as a man of integrity if I should begin to behave as a believer.

Now a man who takes the chance of acting as if he believes, or as if he loves, is taking a dangerous risk. There are three possible outcomes. He can discover that he is a hypocrite and must then suffer his own displeasure with the attempt. Or, secondly, he can slip into a way of living which is comfortable enough so that he will never again pose the radical question about his own integrity. In that case he will live without suffering and without joy because he will have abdicated his own humanity. Finally, he risks being caught up in what he has "tried" and discovering that the faith or love he was trying to lay hold of has laid hold of him. He runs the risk of discovering that tentative commitments have a way of slipping imperceptibly into profound commitments, and that mysteries have a way of seizing us and unfolding before us almost of their own accord.

If a man wondered whether he loved a woman enough to marry her and waited until he was certain of that love before proposing marriage, he would never marry. On the other hand, a man wondering about the strength of his feelings, who decides to begin acting *as if* he did love a woman completely, will soon discover that his attempts are foolish and that he does not love her, or that he loves the pretense so much he has forgotten about the woman, or that in his testing of love he has really fallen in love.

The man who "tries" faith will discover the same thing. Under the best of circumstances, he will find that he has slipped into a deep commitment to the mystery and that the mystery has become one "linchpin" of his life. It is in that discovery, rooted in the decision to try to believe, that we can find the beginning of real prayer. Prayer will be the continuing effort to "try on" faith from day to day, the attempt to discover just how far I can push belief, given my current development in faith and personality. It will be the exercise of the new faculty for knowing — which is faith.

The modern world certainly admits the power of intellectual knowledge but, more and more, modern men are realizing the power of "knowing" that is open only to those who love. Prayer is the work that is done to restore a second way of knowing, faith, to its proper place in the catalogue of man's powers to grasp his life-in-the-world.

Signs And Wonders

If a person were profoundly interested in the question of prayer, he would sooner or later raise the very fundamental question: "How are we able to communicate with God?" In that question, I place the emphasis on the word "we" because there are so many of us. The problem I am trying to deal with is this: how can we begin to describe God's ability to be related in a personal way to so many millions of men and women all over the world? This is a really crucial question for the whole posture of a person's prayer life depends on what he understands to be God's action in the relationship and whether or not that understanding is articulated. As I speak to many people about prayer, I am a little surprised to note that so many of them have no clear notion of what God's own life must be like. With the witness of Scripture, and with twenty centuries of the Christian experience of prayer, every person should have access to some basic notions of how God lives and how He relates to us.

It is not unusual at all to find mature and sophisticated people falling into the common and simplistic conception of God as being basically just like man, only better. In this light, God is seen as living more or less as we do and entering into personal relationships more or less as we do, the only difference being that He is able to do a lot more of it since He is all-powerful. He plans His day as we do, deciding whom He will speak to today and whom He will ignore. He thinks things through and sets out to "surprise" certain people in the course of a given day by giving them signs of His life and presence, signs which are not always clear and which challenge the person to uncover their meaning. What is more, He is doing this in perhaps a few million cases each day. This notion of divine activity is a surprising parallel to the "Santa Claus" legend, which gives so much delight to children at Christmas time. The child believes, unreflectively, that Santa will visit him, and millions of other children, in the course of a single night. Of course, there's a logical problem in the Santa Claus story but very young children don't see it. The child has to picture Santa making all those millions of visits in sequential order, one after another. The story is credible to youngsters because they have no clear notion of time. As they grow older, and achieve some understanding of how long it takes to accomplish some tasks in their own lives, they begin to wonder about Santa Claus. Parents are then forced to explain the problem; they postulate the existence of a small army of "Santa's Helpers" and the story becomes progressively thinner. Even a child's simple faith is strained and soon enough the story loses its power to hold him.

Yet, many adults look at their relationship with God as basically an extension of the "Santa Claus" method of personal visitation. Of course, God is unlimited in His powers so He is not forced to visit us in a sequential order; He is able to deal with us all simultaneously. He leaves a multitude of little personal surprises in our daily lives, one special surprise for each person He has decided He will communicate with each day. That fundamental notion is the underpinning, conscious or unconscious, of a style of religious living which moves a person to search through the ordinary events of a day and look for God's special revelation. It moves people to think of God as a busy sort of person, deciding (almost whimsically) from day to day what remarkable things He will do, or have done, to them. Religious living then becomes a kind of "treasure hunt," a search for profound meaning and revelation in events which other men see as ordinary and insignificant.

What a strange reversal that point of view represents! How different that busy God is from the God Who became man in Jesus! When the time came for Jesus to take leave of His friends, He took the opportunity of their last meal together to offer a summary of His whole life's work and, in making that summary, He did not point to any of His many activities, words and gestures. Instead He said to them, "I will not leave you orphans; I will come back to you. In a short time the world will no longer see me, but you will see me, because I live and you will live. On that day you will understand that I am in my Father and you in me and I in you" (*John 14:18-20*). His parting message is that "on that day," after the Holy Spirit has come, we will see Him "because I live." In summarizing His life and work, He points not to His many activities but to His very existence and tells His disciples that, more than His words and actions, it has been His presence itself that has been the revelation of His Father. In fact, His legacy to them at that Supper is His presence in the bread and wine which become His Body and Blood.

When we make God a busy little creature occupying Himself with the millions upon millions of details in our millions upon millions of lives we do just that: we make Him a *little creature*, a creature of our needs and desires, a creature Who responds to our demand that we be able to see Him in a simple set of activities in our daily lives. But that is the reversal of all that He said and did in Jesus. In Jesus, He took "the condition of a slave" (*Philippians 2:7*), He "became sin for us" (*2 Corinthians 5:21*), He was made to be like us "in all things but sin." And the greatest and most powerful sign of His absolute commitment to our human condition is the sign of His death. In spite of all His great promise and power and in spite of His divinity He was, in the end, a victim of death even as you and I will be its victims. But, finally, He overcame death and gave new life to all.

The death He accepted freely for our sake is not

merely a momentary event; it is not just the split second when His body ceased to operate biologically. His death is the condition in which He lived, the human condition, which leads inexorably to that moment of biological "death." Death is the moment in which a man is apparently cut off from all his potential; all the things he might have done in the world will now go undone for all time. But there are smaller signs of death in all the moments of our living. When I am ill, I am reminded of my mortality because in that condition I am cut off from a certain range of my possibilities. Some of the things I imagine I could do I find I am unable to do because my body cannot reach the potential my mind envisions. Jesus healed the sick precisely to show that He intended to restore man to all of his potential. When I sin I am reminded of my mortality because, in that condition, I am cut off from a certain range of my possibilities; some of the good I imagine I could do I find I am unable to do because in my moral fiber I am inclined away from the potential for good my mind envisions. As St. Paul puts it, "In fact, this seems to be the rule, that every single time I want to do good it is something evil that comes to hand. In my inmost self I dearly love God's Law, but I can see that my body follows a different law that battles against the law which my reason dictates" (*Romans 7:21-23*). Jesus forgave many sinners precisely to show that He intended to restore man to all of his potential.

But, if I look carefully at those instances of "death in life," I will see that they have one thing in common: Jesus worked on them, transformed them symbolically by His healing and forgiveness, but they were other people's problems — He Himself was not a victim of those things, He was not ill and He was not a sinner. But He was a victim of sin and death all of His life; all of His life He suffered from the frustration of sensing His potential was unfulfilled, as surely as we do. And His principle suffering came from His commitment to the human form of communication. Jesus communicated with the men of His world by word and gesture, by the signs which we all use to share ourselves with each other. And, like the rest of us, He failed to transmit the truth of His life through those signs. He did succeed in transmitting the whole truth, but He accomplished that only in His death, His resurrection, and the sending of His Holy Spirit.

Have you ever thought how wonderful it would be to have lived in Christ's time, to have walked with Him and heard His words, and felt His immense compassion and love? Have you ever thought that if only you had that blessing all would be well, and you would have faith enough to move mountains? Have you ever thought that it would be much easier to give yourself to Him completely if only you could have seen and heard Him? If you have thought that, think again. What good did those blessings bring to Peter, whom the Lord loved so deeply — Peter who denied Him three times though he had seen and heard and felt Jesus' deep affection? What good was that experience for the two disciples who were going home to Emmaus on Easter morning disheartened and confused and disappointed because their Lord was dead now? Jesus was a victim of more than the Roman cross and lance. He suffered much more than scourgings and mockery. He suffered the frustration of failure, that all of what He did and said was insufficient to bring to His disciples and beloved friends the one truth He was sent to bring — the truth of "Emmanuel," God is with us.

Here is the provocative contradiction of human communication: every sign we choose to reveal ourselves with obscures as much as it reveals, and Jesus was made a victim of that contradiction for our sake.

Why then, in our age, do we wish to reverse that pattern, to pretend that this contradiction does not exist? Why do we insist that the Lord is making Himself plain in signs and wonders and that all we have to do is keep our eyes and ears open, as if we have more power than the Apostles had? We have the same power the Apostles had: the power to know not what God does, but that He is alive. He does not change whimsically from day to day, offering today one message and tomorrow another. He has not buried Himself in obscure books and accidental events. He is alive and pulsating with the desire to show Himself to us, and that pulsating hunger in Him is the same from day to day. It is not something which is hidden in this or that little event, it is identical with His life. He "does" the same thing each day; He is existing for us, He is being God for us, He is making the total gift of Himself each day to all men. He is not Santa Claus bringing this little present to me today and that little trinket to you. He is the God of Abraham, of Isaac and of Joseph, offering to us precisely what He offered to them: His whole self, His complete presence, His great power. If anyone were to see and receive all that was offered, he would die. And so it is — we do not grasp the full gift except in death, in the beatific vision of the Lord Whom we will meet face to face. In this world we notice only bits and pieces of His self-gift. Today I seem to see His gift of mercy, yesterday I seemed to notice only His terrible justice; today I sense His disappointment in my failures, whereas yesterday I was filled with joy because I knew He loved me for my small successes. But this compartmentalization of God's life is my action, not His. He is not offering me anything different today than yesterday, He has not changed overnight — I have. Today I see more or less than yesterday, not because God is teasing me with something new, but because my eyes and heart are open wider or shut more firmly. I am the child of whimsy, He is the Constant One, the Father Who gives all to all each day.

My prayer must be prayer for my own constancy, for my own patience, for my own growth in the ability to hear as much of God's message of full life as I can on this day. Only a fool, or a pagan, could pray that God would change today to give me more. A Christian knows that God is offering all of His life and presence and power each day. I pray not that God will change, for that is an impossibility, but that I will change and open up more and more of my life, each day, to the fullness of revelation and power He is bringing to me, and to all my brothers and sisters at all times.

The Struggle Of Prayer

To say that prayer is a struggle should be simple enough. Anyone who tries to pray knows that it is difficult and requires patience and a great openness of heart and mind. I hope, eventually, to say something more than what is predictable about the struggle of developing a good prayer life. My ultimate aim, in this chapter, is to demonstrate that the deepest struggle involves the battle with our own expectations and imaginations. But, before I can come to that, I must first speak of some of the more obvious elements of the struggle.

First of all, prayer is a struggle because of the way that we have abused our wonderful gift of language. I know that it is considered quite "the thing" to say that prayer must go far beyond language but, realistically, our prayer must start somewhere and the point of departure is always language. I do, of course, mean to refer to the words that we use as "language" but there is more to it than that. All the processes we go through to prepare ourselves for any activity are "linguistic" because they involve the use of signs and gestures. If I seek out a special place for prayer, or assume a certain posture, or refer to certain feelings and instincts in myself I am acting in a "linguistic" way because I am using signs and symbols to communicate, in this case with myself, and to set up for myself the basic atmosphere of prayer.

The linguistic nature of prayer is an element of struggle because we are so very awkward with language. Our generation has killed words by stretching them beyond all proportion to their initial meaning. How hollow it sounds to say I "love" God when I know that the word "love" is freely applied to everything from the most profound movements of the human heart to my feelings about my breakfast cereal and my toothpaste. There are men who make their living, good livings indeed, by inflating words, by playing on the deep and secret connections words and signs have for us so as to create false needs in us. If you can be convinced that a toothpaste has something to do with "sexiness" then the advertiser, and the seller he represents, will have succeeded in connecting a relatively inconsequential product with the profound, God-created need human beings have for intimacy. If I can convince you that my frivolous aerosol kitchen perfume will dissipate "funny cooking odors" I will be able to tap a well of human respect and the fear of shame in you, tap it

38

just enough to bring forth a trickle of feeling, enough feeling to move you to buy my product. We live in a sea of words, an ocean of communication, and devoted professionals are manipulating language all around us so as to use what is deepest in us to make us buy what we don't need. Jolt after jolt is delivered to our unconscious and preconscious minds, and words are the "electric current" of those manipulative jolts. We have been "oversold," and all those fine words are now inconsequential.

We may want very much to put our feelings into words and to use gestures well to create the atmosphere of peace and prayerfulness, but there is a nagging suspicion at the back of the mind that we are play-acting, that we are doing or saying something we saw or heard in a movie. We don't trust words anymore, not even our own. Recently I heard a talk given by a very talented parish priest in my home diocese. He used a most imaginative and arresting phrase; he said that we have "the language of commitment but a fierce appetite for conformity." What he meant was that we love fine new words and exciting new gestures but that, at the heart of it all, we still mean the same old things. For instance, we love to hear and talk about marriage as "commitment" and "self-gift," but when it comes right down to it, we would much prefer just to be a "husband" or "wife" as society envisions. We love to talk about the "costliness" of love, about the terrible "risks" involved in revealing ourselves to one another but, in the last analysis, we avoid all the costs and risks by simply doing and saying what we're expected to do and say.

That certainly happens in prayer. I can read the Scriptures until my eyes fall out, I can muse over mystical writings until I nearly burst with enthusiasm, but when it comes down to praying myself, my own language just won't convey what I want it to. I'm too awkward with the new words and ideas and I fall back to where I was. The beauty of John of the Cross breaks my heart but my own prayer still isn't much beyond "now I lay me down to sleep"!

Beyond the problems presented by language itself there are even greater difficulties in the quality of reflection represented by our use of language. As a generalization, I offer the observation that we tend to be generally unreflective in our daily lives. We allow most of our experiences to slip by without taking the time to extract from them any meaning beyond the obvious. We lack the patience to reflect on our experiences and to obtain from them any meaning beyond what we were already prepared to receive. For most of us, the horizon of the possibility of our experiences is defined and limited by the time we have reached our late teen years, and our unwillingness to be reflective prevents us from expanding that horizon during the rest of our lives.

Of course, there are times when we are hungry for deeper meanings, times when we cannot afford the luxury of settling for the bits and remnants of other people's reflections which we have stored away in a haphazard fashion long ago. When I am confronted with great tragedy I desperately need a new breakthrough, a new level of understanding. When someone I love dearly dies, or leaves my life in some other way, I sense a heartfelt hunger to understand my experience of loss in a new and more satisfying way. My terror and my loneliness will not be content with old words and old ideas, and I must find new help in putting together the pieces of my life.

In the same way, deep joys call for new reflection. When a man falls in love, or discovers a new fulfillment in his work, his exuberance bursts forth and bubbles over and he is hungry for a new way to understand his joy. When I am filled with new happiness, I am anxious for a new and more reflective way of understanding my experience so that I can store it away for future reflection. A person in love looks tenderly at all the details of the place where he first felt loved so deeply so that he will never forget the moment. He wants to be able to recreate that joy years from now so that he can savor its depth and its satisfaction and its joy.

But there is more than just the ability to recreate the scene of joy or suffering that is at stake. I want to know more deeply what parts of myself, what new qualities of my own being, are being called forth in these experiences so that I can revisit the "place of depth" within myself later on. We are not usually reflective enough to recognize how much power daily events have for awakening new qualities in ourselves, and so we do let those simple joys and sorrows of daily living slip away, consistently losing the opportunity to expand our personal horizons. The person who wants to be prayerful must develop a new sensitivity, a new openness to reflection in his life. If I truly believe that God is alive, if I truly believe that He is con-

41

stantly offering the gift of His entire being to me, then I must be a person of deeply reflective inclinations. You see, to return to the error of "signs and wonders," if I believed that God were communicating with me through disconnected "surprises," through small and mysterious "messages" from day to day, then I wouldn't have to be reflective at all. All I would need, in that case, would be a strong curiosity, a cleverness in solving riddles, and the soul of a detective. But if there really is only *one* God, and if He really is offering *Himself* (rather than secrets *about* Himself) to me each day of my life, then I must have the ability to analyze and sort out my experiences on a very deep level. If my living is a series of isolated and disconnected moments, in some of which God is speaking to me directly and in others He is silent, then I will need to be *alert.* But if He truly is so great, so vast, so immense and so unique that He is able to offer His whole identity to me in the organic unity of my whole life, then I must find deep within myself the center of my own peace, the center of my own identity, the "part" of me which has been made in *His* image and likeness. It will be that deep, peaceful, reflective place within me which is open to His self-offering.

Being reflective implies a high degree of self-possession. A person distracted by questions about his own basic worth, or his acceptance by others and by God, cannot give himself freely to the peace and serenity necessary for real reflection. We must be convinced that we are loveable; we must have assurance that we are secure and accepted before we can be truly prayerful people. Only that assurance can exorcise the fears of the man who doubts himself. As St. John says, "fear is driven out by perfect love" (*1 John 4:18*). But self-possession and assurance are subtle qualities, too easily confused with a most suffocating brand of spiritual pride. A person can be so sure of himself that he leaves no room in his life for the freedom of those around him or for the freedom of God.

Real self-possession makes a man reflective because it is the most hopeful attitude of the human person. When I am assured of my own worth, when I can rely thoroughly on God's love and acceptance of me, then I place all my hope in Him. I am profoundly convinced that all that happens to me is an expression of His love and His saving power; I am certain that all of my experiences are moments of His total self-revelation and self-gift. But if my "self-possession" is the false pride of those who think they know themselves, and the false faith of those who think they know God, then my attitude is not one of hope but one of expectation: I *expect* God to do what seems logical, given the understanding I imagine I have from Scripture, or theology, or whatever.

I remember how shocked I was as a child when I first learned about all the Old Testament prophecies about Christ. My teachers presented the whole picture of prophecy and fulfillment in such a clear and simple manner that I couldn't imagine how the men and women of Jesus' time could have been so stupid and blind and insensitive as to fail to understand that He was the Messiah. But, as I grow older, I begin to sympathize deeply with those people. They just didn't *expect* that the Messiah would be a person like Jesus of Nazareth. Enough years have passed in my life, and enough of my hopes have degenerated into nearly surly expectations, for me to appreciate how blind a person can be to a gift if he is expecting something else. A man of deep self-possession, a man who had truly placed all his hope in God, would be moved by Isaiah's beautiful words: "Here is my servant whom I uphold, my chosen one in whom my soul delights. I have endowed him with my spirit that he may bring true justice to the nations. He does not cry out or shout aloud, or make his voice heard in the streets. He does not break the crushed reed, nor quench the wavering flame" (*Isaiah 42:1-3*). Once men had hoped for salvation from God and were anxious to receive whatever the Lord would offer. With the passage of years, with the loss of the innocence that comes from humble self-possession, with the growth of pride that comes when men believe they are in "special" communication with God, that hope diminished and was replaced by a series of expectations. Men didn't expect the Messiah to be so gentle, so humble, so compassionate, so unobtrusive. Proud as we are, which one of us would be so foolish as to claim that he would not have been victimized by the same lack of trust and openness?

We have a perverse talent for taking each other and God for granted, for imagining we "know" other people. We say we are hopeful, we say we have faith in others and in God. But often enough, what we mean is that we believe in ourselves and our own understanding of other people and of God. Often we mean that we have placed our hope in ourselves and that now we are exuberant enough to be confident in our expectation that others will live up to our expectations of them.

Is there anyone who has never argued bitterly with someone he loved? Haven't we all waited in hope for a loved one to return from anger and estrangement? Haven't we all waited patiently and in suffering, hoping that someone very dear to us would make some sign of forgiveness and affection and renewed love? And haven't we all known times when our own pride strangled our hopes because we have insisted that the other person come to us with the specific signs that we expect him to make? This is how our imaginations and expectations manage to make us blind and deaf; they rob us of the freedom to recognize the spontaneous and unpredictable gifts that people make of themselves; they suffocate the other person with a web of preconceived notions and try to force the other into our patterns of imagining and expecting. I have seen lovers hurt each other deeply because the anxiety of their expectations of each other made them blind to the other's struggle to reveal himself, or herself, in love. I have seen religious people so consumed with their own "piety" and their own presumptions about God and His ways that they were blind to God's unexpected and unpredictable gift of His entire being in their lives.

This degeneration of hope into expectation reflects a most disrespectful way we have of dealing with one another. When the first enthusiasm of love has worn off, when we achieve comfort without real peace and self-esteem without self-possession, we begin reducing the ones we love to things small enough to fit inside our minds. We begin to imagine that we know others so well that we no longer need to suffer the pain that hope invariably brings. We come to feel that we can predict what the other will think, feel, want, and offer. "For we must be content to hope that we shall be saved — our salvation is not in sight, we should not have to be hoping for it if it were — but, as I say, we must hope to be saved since we are not saved yet — it is something we must wait for with patience (*Romans 8:24-25*). We do not hope for what is seen, least of all for the things we can see in ourselves, in our own imaginations. Our hope is the risky commitment of ourselves to the loving good will of another. Prayer is a great struggle for us because we shy away from hope, and would rather spend our time and energy developing our expectations. Prayer is a struggle because we would rather have the roots of our security in ourselves than in One Whom we cannot pretend to "know."

Familiarity
With The Lord

As is the case in any living relationship, one of
the reasons why we are willing, and even anxious,
to endure the struggle of prayer in our life with the
Lord is that we are anxious to grow in familiarity
with the Other. It is important to note that this
growth in familiarity is *one of the reasons* for our
willingness to endure the struggle, not the goal of
the struggle itself. In some relationships, I suppose,
familiarity is the goal, but those are most often
possessive and self-serving relationships. In a true
and deep relationship of love, mere familiarity will
never do; lovers want to penetrate each other's
very being, to achieve a quality of mutual presence
that is independent of familiarity. When I have
passed the stage of merely recognizing mutual
needs and resources in a friendship, I am ready to

take the step of truly committing myself to the other.

Being familiar with the other, and with his ways, is one building block in the overall relationship which is being created by our mutual desire to share life together. A key element of the familiarity which is proper to love, to the deepest relationships between human beings and to our relationship with the Lord, is that it must be a respectful familiarity. I suppose that everyone has heard the saying "familiarity breeds contempt." The kind of familiarity which breeds contempt cannot be endured in love, especially in our love for the Lord.

Familiarity does breed contempt when it is superficial, when it concerns itself with an unreflective analysis of the things the other person does. If a person who does not love me saw me in my weakest and most human moments he might feel contempt for me. He might think, "Who is this man that he should present himself publicly to speak about God and religion when, in fact, he is no more religious than I am!" But if a person already loved and valued me, then a growth in familiarity, such as the observation of my most human weaknesses, might very well breed deeper affection rather than contempt.

Let us move now to a very difficult analogy. Is there some way that familiarity can breed contempt in a person's dealing with God? Suppose a person who does not yet love the Lord were to take the time to examine one aspect of His life. Let us take, for example, the fact that the Lord seems to permit evil in the world. Couldn't that person observe the suffering that is experienced in the world and say, "Who is this 'God' that He should be presented as someone to be loved and adored when He does nothing to relieve these great sufferings, when He permits them all to continue?" The familiarity which is a part of prayer and a proper building block in my relationship with God is not this superficial observation of what God "does"; is a profoundly reflective recognition of who God is.

Growing in familiarity with God requires that we invest time, patience, and a measure of creativity in coming to know who He is. We must try to come to know and love the things of the Lord. The kind of familiarity which we are seeking is the kind that will move us to see things spontaneously as He sees them, and to respond to life spontaneously out of the Christian tradition rather than out of our own prejudices. What we are hoping for is that one day we will find it natural to turn to the Lord in all moments of our life, and to look to Him for His rich gifts in all that we need. As St. Paul puts it, "All belong to the same Lord who is rich enough, however many ask his help, for everyone who calls on the name of the Lord will be saved" (*Romans 10:12-13*). St. Paul suggests that this "calling on the name of the Lord" is something much more than just saying, "Lord, Lord." Later on in the letter to the Romans, he says that a community which is calling on the name of the Lord is anxious to share this blessing with others, so anxious that it will send out preachers to spread the news of God's power. "But they will not ask his help unless they believe in him, and they will not believe in him unless they have heard of him, and they will not hear of him unless they get a preacher, and they will never have a preacher unless one is sent" (*Romans 10:14-15a*). This "calling on the name of the Lord," then, is a complex thing. In a way, St. Paul uses the phrase to summarize the whole Christian life, the message that the Church must pass on to those who do not believe: we are to send out preachers so that others may hear and believe and thus come to "call on the name of the Lord" themselves.

The community which "calls on the name of the Lord" is one which has true familiarity with him; it is a group that spontaneously draws from the Christian tradition in that it turns to the Lord in all things. There are several elements of faith-living which such a community must possess: it must have good liturgical celebrations, it must be a reflective community with high regard for the Scriptural witness, and it must be a group which exercises responsible concern for its members.

Good liturgical celebrations are those in which a community recognizes that God is taking the initiative to reveal Himself to them through sacramental rites. When I speak of the quality of liturgy, I am not referring to the music used, or the physical setting, or the ability of the preacher to move his listeners — I am speaking of the commitment of the people of the community to be attentive and self-possessed during the liturgical celebration so that the Lord can have the opportunity to do the work He intended to do when He established liturgical actions.

When I speak of the reflective nature of the community, I am not only referring to the fact that a community must have its scholars (scholarship is important, especially in dealing with a thing so difficult as the Scriptures), but reflection is far more than mere scholarship. It is an attitude of humility and patience; it is the style of living of those who are convinced that life does mean something, convinced that the meaning of human life is always the same as the revelation of God in Scripture and in the Church.

Finally, responsible community concern is a very complex reality. Perhaps I can best illustrate this by relating a pair of experiences I had recently. Two elderly friends of mine died in the space of ten days. I attended both funerals and the contrast between them was striking. The first funeral was held in a large, urban church. Some of the family members were "good organizers" and, when they realized that there were going to be many people at the cemetery for the burial, they decided that they should relieve the man's widow of the burden of worrying about accommodating the guests after the burial. When I had said the last prayer at the graveside, one of the family members announced that a lunch would be served for all of us at a local restaurant. The restaurant was not ostentatious, and the meal was plain, but the gesture was beautiful. The widow had nothing to worry about in the social situation, and those who had been at the cemetery were treated well, and felt that their attention had been noticed and valued. The second funeral was for an elderly woman who had died in a small town in eastern Long Island. The neighborhood was almost rural. The day of the burial was an awful, rain-soaked day and I saw how uncomfortable the widower was when he realized that, after the burial in the little graveyard, there were twenty or thirty people standing in the rain, most of them with a long trip home ahead of them. He told us that his little house was in a shabby condition since his wife had become so ill a few weeks before, but that he would like us all to come back there with him. He said he was sure that we could make some coffee, and perhaps get some cold cuts for a light meal. Everyone was very moved by his offer, and a few of us started talking about where we could go to get some food for the small crowd. We decided to go to the house first to see what would be needed. When we arrived at the house we were very surprised and very deeply moved. In the few hours since my friend had left his house for the funeral home that morning, a group of his neighbors had come in, cleaned and tidied the place up beautifully, and brought with them plates and plates of sandwiches and other food for any guests who might come back to the house after the burial.

Now in both cases the same effect was achieved. The guests at both funerals were made to feel comfortable, and their needs were met. In both cases the bereaved person was relieved of the burden of looking after practical necessities. The impressive difference for me was that in the second case, the attentions of the neighbors seemed to be derived from a spontaneous sense of common responsibility for a man in need. I do not wish to detract from the family members who were so compassionate in the first case, I only want to say that the neighbors in the second case did what no one would expect them to do — they gave of themselves, not out of concern for *their* guests in an awkward social situation, but out of spontaneous love and good will for a member of their community.

I don't mean to reduce "responsible community concern" to mere organization of "soup brigades" to help people out of awkward situations, but little touches like that are a simple sign of a community's style of living together. It's not so much that responsible community living goes beyond those small touches, rather it "gets behind them," reflective consciousness of the source of such kindnesses. The responsible community reflects on its common needs and celebrates them in liturgy. It recognizes that the "community" is a living community composed of persons with concrete needs who have been formed into a community by the doctrine and faith they share. It also recognizes that the community to which we belong is comprised of more than the people we see in need and with gifts around us. The Church extends all over the whole world. What is more, the Church is not merely the obviously "living" community of those in the world sharing faith with each other. As a matter of fact, the vast majority of those who have "called on the name of the Lord" are now dead. What I mean to suggest here is that keeping faith with the community requires more than good manners, and more than orthodox religious beliefs, and even more than strong efforts to celebrate liturgy well. It requires the realization that we are heirs of many generations of faith, that what we believe comes to us from Christ through the efforts and witness and mediation of men and women who have struggled to live the faith through many ages.

I suppose that it is true that in the recent past Christians, and Catholics in particular, have tended to overgeneralize about "the Church." We have spoken so institutionally that we have failed to identify the Church as a community of believers past and present. I am still meeting people today who cannot grasp the importance of public worship, and they fail in this because they fail to understand the Church as community. But I am fearful of an overreaction to this problem, of a backlash that would focus so precisely on the visible local community that it would cut us off altogether from the roots of our faith. If I am to grow in a genuine familiarity with the Lord, then I must be attentive to all the ways He has chosen to reveal Himself. I am deeply disturbed when I meet groups of Christian people who are meeting together in an attempt to grow in faith without the benefit of the work and spiritual richness of past ages. I am deeply disturbed when I hear groups of people speaking as if they had only just discovered the religious life. I am reminded of the way adolescents talk when they fall in love. They are taking their first tentative steps on the risky journey out of themselves, and are convinced that no one has ever walked that way before. Every adult would like to reach out to such youngsters and offer help. We would like to share our experiences with them and save them the pain of making the same mistakes others have made. But we smile at them, we recognize that they are immature, and we leave them to their own devices, hoping they will not be so deeply hurt by their isolation that they will never really learn to love. But there is really no excuse for adolescence in matters of faith. What a great fool one would have to be to imagine that he were experiencing God in a way so deeply personal that no one could be of help to him on the journey. Of course my experience of God is unique, as unique as all my experiences are because they are mine. But it is the uniqueness of my personality which makes them different. I am not discovering a new form of love, only the "Alan Placa" way of loving. I am not having a radically new experience of God, only the "Alan Placa" way of confronting the experience of the One Who has not changed since He first breathed life into Adam, made His promises to Abraham, gave His law to Moses, spoke to the heart of Jeremiah, met Peter by the sea, and shared Himself with the thousands of saints who have lived since.

One certain way for me to grow in genuine familiarity with Him, in a familiarity which will convince me of my own fragility rather than breed prideful contempt, is to immerse myself in the Church, in her ways and experiences, in her strengths and weaknesses. To commit myself to the Church is to connect myself to man's great project of responding with authenticity and integrity to God's gift of Himself.

Sharing
The Life Of God

The word "sharing" is one of the most popular in the modern vocabulary. It is nestled regally in the golden ark of the covenant which is the dictionary of those who worship jargon. It is kept company in that holy of holies by its confrères "dialogue," "encounter," "sensitivity," "experience," and "witness," and a legion of lesser angels. I have nothing against any of the realities signified by those words. I am only put off when I suspect that people seek sharing and dialogue and encounter and the rest for their own sake. In other words, before I get together with others to "share" with them, I want to be quite certain that I have something to share. Sometimes I suspect that people come together to pray in groups because they haven't the faintest idea what it means to pray alone. I am very suspicious of people who claim they have found God in their sharing with others in a way they had never found Him before. I remember the story of the blind men who were terrified when they came across an elephant one day in the jungle. Their terror was due to the fact that they didn't know what it was. They decided to get together to examine the situation and share their insights. One man walked up to the elephant and reached out and grabbed its leg. He put his arms around the leg and felt it for a long time. Finally, he told his friends he had solved the problem: it was only a tree in front of them. Another man took hold of the elephant's tail, examined it with his fingers, and laughed. "How foolish we are," he said, "to be afraid! I have examined the thing, and it is only a rather large worm!" A third blind man had gotten hold of the animal's trunk, and he told his friends not to be so sure. "You may think this is only a large worm, but if you ask me, we're up against a snake here!" While all of the men were examining the elephant, each from his own personal point of view, and each arriving at the wrong conclusion, the animal got bored and walked off. Finally, another blind man walked forward to the place where the elephant had been standing. He kept walking until he came up against a blank wall. He ran his hands along the wall, which was very high and very rough, and ran in terror. As he passed his friends he called out to them, "Run, all of you! That thing is an elephant!"

Of course they were all fools. Too prideful to admit that they lacked the equipment to understand what they were confronting, they decided to pool their incompetence. In the end they arrived at no truth at all. They had "shared," but they really had nothing *to* share. When I speak of sharing prayer, I don't mean getting together like frightened doves in a storm to exorcise the fear of our own ignorance. By sharing, I mean the whole process that begins with the hard work of opening my mind and heart to God and then, finally, bringing what I have found of God's love forward for the edification of my fellow believers.

There are really two kinds of sharing involved in prayer: first, there is the sharing in God's life which is the Christian life; second, there is our sharing of what we have experienced of the Lord with each other.

The first step, the sense of sharing in God's life, is certainly the more difficult. As religious people, we must realize that a strong sense that we are living the life of Christ is absolutely essential to us. Certainly it is essential for whatever work we do which can be considered "ministerial." If I have not a deep life shared with God, if I am not a profoundly prayerful person in regular contact with the Lord, then I am a sham, and those to whom I minister will eventually know that. But that shared life is also essential to my own sense of integrity: I must feel, from day to day, that there is something real to my living the life of faith, that in some way I have begun to live a new life in the Lord. St. Paul puts it most dramatically when he says, "I have been crucified with Christ, and I live now not with my own life but with the life of Christ who lives in me. The life I now live in this body I live in faith: faith in the Son of God who loved me and who sacrificed himself for my sake" (*Galatians 2:19b-20*).

But, I firmly believe that no one can sense the depth of life which God is living within him until he has first experienced the frustration of seeking that life out. It is not until I have become completely convinced that there is no way that I can know the life of God that I am ready to learn of that life from God Himself. Spend a moment reflecting on the story of the rich young man who walked away from Jesus, and take a lesson from the story for your own life of prayer: "Jesus said [to the rich young man], 'If you wish to be perfect, go and sell what you own and give the money to the poor, and you will have treasure in heaven; then come, follow me.' But when the young man heard these words he went away sad, for he was a man of great wealth. Then Jesus said to his disciples, 'I tell you solemnly, it will be hard for a rich man to enter the kingdom of heaven. Yes, I tell you again, it is easier for a camel to pass through the eye of a needle than for a rich man to enter the kingdom of heaven.' When the disciples heard this they were astonished. 'Who can be saved, then?' they said. Jesus gazed at them. 'For men,' he told them, 'this is impossible; for God everything is possible' " (*Matthew 19:21-26*). The disciples did not miss the essential point of what Jesus had meant; this was not merely a condemnation of riches as a source of distraction, it was a very harsh saying about the difficulty of salvation. And Jesus does not mince words in describing the difficulty involved: " . . . for men this is impossible." In the spiritual life, all things are impossible for men and all things are possible for God. It is the man who is exhausted with his own search for salvation who is ready to receive God's gentle word of saving power. If I want to know the real consolation of prayer, I will first have to exhaust myself trying every method I can discover, and discovering that they all fail. I will have to taste the frustration of that failure before my pride will be silent enough to allow me to hear God's voice calling.

The frustration of the failure of my own attempts to pray is a bitter thing. I remember a movie I saw years ago, a British comedy. It never achieved much popularity, and I have long since forgotten the title and the names of the actors. But there is one scene I will never forget. A man is on his first visit to a psychiatrist's office. Doctor and patient are chatting calmly and urbanely. After a while the doctor confesses that he can't understand why the man has come to him, since he can see no signs of pathology in anything the man has said or done. The patient explains that his wife asked him to come. When the doctor asks why, the man explains, "I suppose it was because I told her that I am God." The psychiatrist perks up, "uh-huh's" a few times, and asks the man to explain himself. The patient goes on, "For years I tried to pray. After a while I discovered what most people discover when they try to pray: I discovered that I was just talking to myself. Finally, I drew the logical conclusion: that since in prayer I was talking to myself, I must be God!" The scene, of course, was funny, and the man's conclusion sounds a bit mad. But the frustration he is reporting is quite ordinary. In comedy, that frustration may push people beyond the limits of sanity, but in ordinary living it either pushes them outside of the life of faith completely, or else brings them to the door of true prayer.

The very heart of Judaeo-Christian revelation is this insight: that in the dealings between God and man it is always God Who takes the initiative. All religious people begin with the affirmation of God's existence. We part ways when we come to the question, "Given the truth of the statement that God exists, what relevance does His existence have to my life?" Or, to put it another way, "How is the chasm between God and man bridged?" Every pagan faith has answered in the same way: communication between God and man is established by some initiative of man. Incantations, holy writings, sacred rituals, ethical codes, mystical formulas: these are the routes which pagan men have undertaken on the journey to God. Some have believed ethical living to be the route to salvation; they maintain that if they live ethically perfect lives, God will be obliged to "save" them, to draw them to Himself. Others are committed to the search for "mystical" experiences in the conviction that by their efforts they can transcend the world of nature and insinuate themselves into God's pure, spiritual realm. In whatever shape it takes, paganism begins from the same point of departure: it is man's responsibility to seek out the secrets of God, and having discovered those secrets, it is man's responsibility to establish contact with God. By becoming God-like himself, man achieves his own ultimate salvation and union with God.

The Christian insight is precisely the opposite of

the pagan. In Judaeo-Christian revelation it is always God Who takes the initiative. In the history of the Jews, in the lives and works of the prophets, and finally in the life and death and resurrection of Christ, it is God Who moves first towards man, communicating with him on his own level. The Christian does not achieve his own salvation by becoming "God-like"; it is God Who actually does become a man in order to establish the union between Himself and men. Our life of prayer must follow the same pattern: we must pass through the "paganism" of imagining that prayer is our work, and face the truth that God is still taking the initiative to communicate with us. I must stop and recognize the fact that my futile efforts to "know" God are being met constantly by God's perfect act of knowing me.

It is simple to point out the fact that God's identity is a mystery. But for that matter, so is my own identity. I have already spoken of "self-possession" as an essential virtue for the person who would be prayerful. But only a shallow and foolish man would imagine that he is in complete possession of himself, and only a very dull man is never surprised by his own reactions. There is a depth within us which is revealed gradually as we come up against new experiences and situations. There is a "secret" concerning my own identity, not only God's. I think St. John is speaking about that "secret" in a highly symbolic way when he says, in the Book of Revelation, "If anyone has ears to hear, let him listen to what the Spirit is saying to the churches: to those who prove victorious I will give the hidden manna and a white stone — a stone with a new name written on it, known only to the man who receives it" (*Revelation 2:17*). Deep within me there is a place where I am truly myself, a secret place which no one can enter except me and God, and I do not undertake that risky journey often.

You see, the real breakthrough to prayer comes when I sense deep frustration in my attempt to know the secret of God's identity and when I then realize that all the while, through all of my futile efforts to know Him, He has been hidden in that deeply secret place within me, knowing the secret of my identity fully and loving it. Seeking the Lord, finding Him, and choosing to be in His presence are not things we can undertake on our own initiative: "You did not choose me, no, I chose you; and I commissioned you to go out and to bear fruit, fruit that will last; and then the Father will give you anything you ask him in my name" (*John 15:16*). I can only understand real contemplation when I have failed at it; when I have failed in all my efforts to contemplate the mystery of God's life, I am ready to recognize the real contemplation which is going on in my life — not my contemplation of God, but God's perfect contemplation of me.

I do share in God's life, and I can reflect on that fact and grasp it in an intellectual way. I can know about the mystery of biological life and contemplate its possible sources. I can understand the hopelessness of human life without God, and know that He gives hope, hope for eternal life. I can understand the gift of my baptism and the price Christ has paid to give me new life. But there is a great gap between understanding these things and feeling them, between the knowledge of life and the experience of it. A man can know much about philosophy from books without ever having suffered what the philosopher suffered in formulating his vision and his insights. A man can know a great deal about the human body, but until he has seen the sufferings the body can endure and has helped to heal those sufferings, he is no physician. An artist can imagine how the body works, but the burning desire to know it fully, so as to portray it realistically, drove Michelangelo to want to see within the body and understand its muscles and bones and mechanisms, to experience in his own life what he could only guess at from other people's representations. I must know more than that God has given me life, and that He continues to share it with me. I must be profoundly convinced in my feelings and experiences that what I know to be true is real. And that conviction will only overtake me when I have seen the futility of my own attempts, and the peaceful perfection of God's act of living within me.

Sharing The Experience Of Prayer

The second kind of sharing which is part of the life of prayer, the process of sharing our prayer life with other human beings, is less subtle than the actual sharing of life with God but it is more dangerous. There is the obvious danger of the blind men around the elephant, but there are other dangers as well. I would suspect that one of the most pressing of modern dangers is the one that arises when people *substitute* shared prayer for private prayer. When that happens, shared prayer becomes a vacuous and self-serving experience. Anyone who has prayed with a group has met some individuals who use the group to execute a kind of psychological relief which they cannot experience anywhere else in their lives. The device operates in this way: I have something I wish to tell you, another human being; it is some terrible secret, some buried guilt, some deep yearning, some private thing which no one loves me enough to listen to; I will come to your group and I will unburden my soul "to God," I will share my secret with Him, and if you should happen to "overhear" it, so much the better. The man I mentioned earlier who thought he was God was judged insane because in prayer he was talking to himself. What will we say of someone who in prayer is talking to other people? Is that person crazy, or merely pitiable because he has not discovered more conventional ways for communicating with his fellow human beings? Shouldn't our hearts go out to him for what he has suffered: that nowhere on earth has he found another human being willing to love him enough to hear his secret joys and sorrows?

That perception may move me to prayer, but it must not be thought that the man is praying. He has cried out to other men in his loneliness, and he may be inviting them to lead him to God, but he has not yet come to know the Lord and His power. The matter would be very simple if we could believe that there are some people who are always in that weak condition, and that there are others who are never in that situation. But that is not the truth. There is some of that weakness in all of us. My "spiritual life" is not a matter of which I can speak univocally, it is not of one homogenous consistency. There are weak, soft spots scattered among the strengths of my life in the Spirit. And that is the danger of groups that share prayer. At any given moment, how can I be sure that we are sharing prayer and not simply the human urge to be heard by other men?

The heart of the problem is the fact that there is really a very fine line between spiritual insight and pure imagination. God is Spirit, He is invisible, and the powers I must use to know and understand Him are invisible, spiritual powers. These powers are close enough to imagination to make distinguishing them from imagination a risky business. Think how often our power of imagination distorts our knowledge of one another. How often I have been blind to the goodness of another person because in my imagination I had already decided that he was evil. How often I have been blind to the hurtful and selfish things another person did because I loved that person, and in my imagination had decided he could do no wrong. And we have bodies and words and gestures of protest with which to defend ourselves! I can insist to you that you have misunderstood and wrongly judged me. I can patiently demonstrate your errors to you. How much easier it would be to "mistake" God, to build up imaginative pictures of Him which are self-serving but untrue. I know a man who claims to be a very religious man — you know men like him, people who say they believe deeply in God, but have no use for churches or organized religion or formal prayer. They "pray always," they say. The man I am thinking of really does spend a great deal of time doing what he calls "praying." I know for a fact that he never undertakes an important project or makes a serious decision unless he has first consulted God. The thing that amazes me and makes me so very jealous of him is the fact that God never disagrees with him. The God I am coming to know has the distasteful habit of disagreeing with me and correcting my ideas all the time. I certainly begin to suspect that my friend is putting himself into firm contact with his own imagination, and not with God. I suspect that what he calls "prayer" the rest of us would call "quiet reflection" and "thinking things through."

Whether I am praying alone or with others, I must be sure that I am contacting the Lord of heaven and earth, and not just the common sense and creativity He has placed in me as signs of His life. This is the real point of sharing prayer: that I must be willing to expose what I have experienced to the scrutiny of the whole Church. I must bring my own private prayer life to the Church and ask her to confirm what is good, and to help me root out what is not good. I must ask her to affirm me in the areas where I have come to know the Lord she has known for two thousand years, and I must ask her to correct me when I have discovered only my own will and my own imagination of "how things ought to be."

When I seek out a group to share my prayer life with, I must be sure that the group is large enough to be of help to me. I must be sure that the whole Church is participating in the group's meetings. I must be sure that we will not be blind men leading other blind men into deeper darkness. I must be sure that there are honest men and women present, people who will be willing to support me when I am in touch with the truth, and to be skeptical and correct me when I stray from the truth; people who will be wise and holy and humble enough to be able to distinguish my successes from my failures. If they are to do that then they must be willing to invite a lot of people into the group. The leaders of the Church must be there, at least through their writings and the official teachings, and our group must listen attentively, respectfully, and intelligently to what they say. The best thinkers of the Church, those living and those long dead, must also be invited to participate — we cannot pretend that we are the first group ever to have wondered about God, or to have tried to pray, or to have sought a deeper relationship with God and with fellow Christians. We must also invite what Father Karl Rahner calls the *ur-kirche* to our group. That phrase is poorly translated into English by the expression "primitive Church," but it really means the generation of faith which produced the writings which the Church has canonized as the New Testament. The word *kirche* means "church," and the best way I can describe the meaning of the particle *ur-* is by example. When Goethe was preparing to write his great play *Faust*, he first wrote a much shorter poem. In this poem he included all of the significant characters, events, and feelings which were to make up the long play. He called the poem "ur-Faust." In a highly concentrated, economical form he had already prepared all that would appear in the play. The play itself would simply be an expansion of the poem. The same is true of the "primitive Church." There is present in the experience of that generation of faith all of the identity of the Christian faith. As history unfolds itself, we are discovering more and more of the implications of their experience of Christ and His Church as we come into contact with new events, personalities, and problems. But the essence of the Church's identity, in a highly concentrated and economical form, is present in that *ur-kirche* and in the New Testament, the record of her experience of the Lord in sacrament and community.

Furthermore, we have the same life of sacraments and public worship available to us which was the life of the *ur-kirche*. All of these elements — church teaching, sound theological opinion, the Scriptural witness, and the ever-present fact of liturgical experience — are necessary for healthy group-life since they are the criteria against which we must measure the authenticity of our own experiences. Christ is true to His promise, He has not "left us orphans" (*cf. John 14:18*). He has not left us to the darkness of our own minds, or to the loneliness of our own private struggles. He remains with us through His Spirit, the soul of His bride, the Church. When we meet together *as the Church*, we are in His presence, and He will show us the truth through the actions of His Spirit. Sometimes those actions will be remarkable, but ordinarily they will be, well, quite ordinary! He will move for us as He always has, in Scripture, in teaching, in theological reflection, and in liturgical worship. He will be the gift of the Father, the Spirit Who prays in us, when we are one with the Church.

I love to reflect upon one particular experience of the Church reported in the New Testament. I love to think of the "cenacle," the upper room in which the apostles shared the Last Supper with the Lord. Of course, the image of the Supper itself is very beautiful, but I am especially moved by the way the disciples lived and met to pray in that room after Jesus had risen from the dead, and after He had returned to His Father. Here is the description of that experience from the Acts of the Apostles: "When they had reached the city they went to the upper room where they were staying; there were Peter and John, James and Andrew, Philip and Thomas, Bartholomew and Matthew, James son of Alphaeus and Simon the Zealot, and Jude son of James. All these joined in continuous prayer, together with several women, including Mary the mother of Jesus, and with his brothers" (*Acts 1:13-14*). It takes a small sense of drama, but I love to imagine what they must have experienced there together. Their Lord had risen from the dead, giving them new hope, but now He left them. He had told them He would not return until the end. They were left to decide what they would do. Much of what they did and said must have been aimed at giving mutual support and encouragement in faith. They must have recalled their experiences with the Lord, and each must have been able to add his own story to the growing sense of mission and confidence. They prayed together, they corrected one another's faulty recollections, and spent time putting their common experience in order so that it could be the source of their strength. The Holy Spirit was there among them leading them in prayer and showing them the truth of Christ.

When we have groups coming together, they must come with the intention of imitating that first "group" in the cenacle. They must draw on the collected wisdom of the Church to encourage and support one another in the act of faith. Each member must feel confident to bring his own experience to the whole group, exposing himself to the group and its many sources of truth. The confidence with which one comes to the group is not based on any assurance of acceptance, it is based on the assurance that the group will tell the truth, the truth which the Lord gives it in Scripture, in church teaching, in sound theology, in sacramental celebration, and in community living.

The Culture Of Prayer

Up to the present, I have concentrated on the interior and personal aspects of prayer, with only a few passing references to the way conditions outside oneself can help or hinder the process. In fact, it is my ultimate purpose to speak of a very specific way of enriching private prayer. But we have reached the point where we must face the question of the influence of our surroundings and general culture on the person who is attempting to live a life of prayer.

For the purposes of our search for deeper roots for the life of prayer, I will define "culture" as *the externalization and socialization of the four basic areas of man's life: the physical, the emotional, the intellectual and the spiritual.* It is my contention that a person's ability to pray well depends, in its roots, on the way he is able to organize these basic areas of life within himself, to externalize their power in word and action, and to share them with others. I may as well say at the outset that I feel strongly that our contemporary secular culture does not help, and in many ways positively militates against, the process of coordinating these basic aspects of life. In my judgment, our society has managed to alienate us from our own deepest longings, and Christ's admonition that we should "belong to the world no more than I belong to the world" (*John 17:14*) becomes more critical day by day. The purely contemplative life functions as a condemnation of secular culture precisely by proclaiming its radical love for each and every element of the created world and, at the same time, rejecting the cultural matrix into which contemporary society attempts to force creation. This witness against culture is saved from empty negativism only in so far as it is offered in the same spirit of brokenhearted compassion with which Jesus wept over Jerusalem when He said, "Jerusalem, Jerusalem, you that kill the prophets and stone those who are sent to you! How often have I longed to gather your children, as a hen gathers her chicks under her wings, and you refused!" (*Matthew 23:37*).

We who are not pure contemplatives must live "in the world, but not of it," and we must be in dialogue with our culture. But our dialogue must proceed out of strength, and from a profound urge to "gather" the children of this world and all the elements of creation into a new order, a new creation. In the second part of this book I will outline a method of contemplative prayer for use by individuals and small groups. This method is meant to be expressive of a "new culture," a new climate, a new order of things in which the elements of the created world are brought into a new harmony. Prayer is the beginning of that new harmony because it is true knowledge of God. To know God is to know the world He has made, and to know the order and the rhythms He had in mind in creating the world. The prophet Isaiah speaks poetically of that secret order hidden in the heart of God:

> "The wolf lives with the lamb,
> the panther lies down with the kid,
> calf and lion cub feed together
> with a little boy to lead them.
> The cow and the bear make friends,
> their young lie down together.
> The lion eats straw like the ox.
> The infant plays over the cobra's hole;
> into the viper's lair
> the young child puts his hand.
> They do no hurt, no harm,
> on all my holy mountain,
> for the country is filled with the knowledge of
>   Yahweh
> as the waters swell the sea"

(Isaiah 11:6-9).

Before proceeding to the description of the method of prayer which I will propose, I must first outline the ways in which our culture has alienated us from our roots, and made Isaiah's vision of peace and harmony a foolish-sounding dream.

Finally, I will have to suggest a way back to the Lord.

1. Our Alienation from the Physical World:

The physical world around us is pulsing with rhythms and patterns of its own living force. The seasons change and each change implies something new for the earth. Each day runs its course into night, and the change from light to darkness is like a voice that calls nature into new action. A forest by day teems with life as animals seek their food and as vegetation drinks in the sunlight which gives it growth. When darkness comes, the tempo of the forest changes, the creatures of daylight seek rest and shelter while other animals take their place seeking out the dark for food-gathering and life-activity. But I have no part in that life or in those rhythms. The changes in the seasons mean little or nothing to me. The dead of winter calls nature to its cycle of rest, but it only calls me to my furnace, to see to it that my ideal climate is maintained regardless of nature. Outside my house the summer heat is the setting for nature's busiest growth; inside, I adjust my air conditioner in my unreflective, fully mechanized protest against nature's cycles. Day and night, light and darkness mean nothing to me. I light up the night so that I can work and play in it as if it were day, and I shut out the morning's brightness so that I can take my rest, finish my "good night's sleep" according to my own clocks, not in time with nature's rhythm.

"From the beginning until now the entire creation, as we know, has been groaning in one great act of giving birth; and not only creation, but all of us who possess the first fruits of the Spirit, we too groan inwardly as we wait for our bodies to be set free" (*Romans 8:22-23*). We may know this, but we have exercised all our ingenuity and marshaled all our technology in our efforts to insulate ourselves from nature's birth-pangs; it is not so much that we want our bodies to be set free as that we want to be set free from our bodies — to be independent of nature's claim on us. Some men may see virtue in these efforts to escape nature's hold, and I would have to be the first to admit my own dependence on technology and its comforts. But I must also admit that the farther I run from the laws of nature and from her rhythms, the farther I find myself from the Law-giver, the Creator of nature. A healthy climate for prayer demands a healthy respect for the body and for the world of nature into which it is placed by its Creator. To pray well is not to escape the body, not to "tell yourself you have to bring Christ down — as in the text: 'Who will go up to heaven?' or that you have to bring Christ back from the dead — as in the text: 'Who will go down to the underworld?' " (*Romans 10:6-7*). To pray well is, first of all, to know that the body is "the temple of the living God" (*2 Corinthians 6:16*), that the body's life, immersed in the world of created nature, must be known and loved and used wisely as a source of the knowledge of God. We have not to escape the body to find the Lord, for we know that "The word, that is the faith we proclaim, is very near to you, it is on your lips and in your heart" (*Romans 10:8*).

2. *Our Alienation from Our Emotions:*

What can I be planning to say here? Can it be that I am going to tell you that we are too cold, too emotionless? Could I possibly be about to tell you that we Americans are overly intellectual and rational, and that we are afraid of our feelings? If I did that, what a wonderful example it would be of the way language so often fails to keep up with experience. The least of our worries today should be the fear that we will be overly intellectual or rational. If anything, we are drowning in a sea of emotions and non-logic. We have come dangerously near to being "sensitized" and "encountered" and "experienced" and "liberated" and "revealed" and "shared" to death. The "emotionless American" is a straw man who had his stuffing finally knocked out somewhere between the "sensitivity groups" and the "siege of Chicago"; his straw is lying rotting on the floors of analysts' offices from coast to coast.

Our society isn't alienating us from our emotions by forbidding their display, it is making us nauseous by rubbing our noses in them. It isn't that we haven't the courage to reveal our deepest emotions, the problem is that we have uncovered so much triviality with so much drama that we have forgotten the way into our true selves. To hell with "hang ups"! To darkest Hades with everyone's "own thing"! To the deepest, coldest pit of hell with all the trivial neuroses that crowd all our minds as surely as bacteria fight over air space. They're all there, some very harmful, some quite delightful, and they aren't worth the sound and fury we raise over them! To love another person, to need another deeply: that's an emotion. To be afraid of losing love and to be willing to suffer to keep it: that's an emotion worthy of the name. To know deep down that there is a secret to my being, and that I need others to help me discover that secret; to hunger for an unfailing presence that knows me and loves me without qualification; to want to be affirmed in the center of my being; to need the gentle loving touch of One Who is sure and beyond change: those are our deepest feelings and our culture has alienated us all from them. To pray well is not to indulge in group hysteria that makes me free enough to say what nobody cares about anyway; to pray well is not to have the "courage" to fall out into the waiting arms of the circle of my peers who are as weak as I am. To pray well is to know that I can fall inward, deep into my own being, and that I will find there the ground of all Being, the Lord Who made me and my peers; it is to know that the fall into myself is not an escape from reality, but a journey into the one place where I can meet myself, my Lord, and my brothers and sisters in reality and honesty.

3. *Our Alienation from Our Intellect:*

The marvelous technology of our age has taught those who care about such things a great deal about the electro-chemical processes by which the human brain observes, stores and recalls data. But somehow in the technological shuffle we have lost the sense of who is in control of that marvelous organism, the brain. Common sense reveals a deep faith in a power of knowing which is beyond the brain every time a person says the words "*my* brain." When I speak of "*my* brain," and "*my* mind," and "*my* body," I am affirming my conviction that *I* am something beyond what is visible and measurable about me. Although my common-sense speech may affirm my faith in my own self-possession, my experiences do not verify that claim. The human intellect is a complicated reality, like a house with many floors. Our culture has filled its attic, and its basement, and a lot of the floors that were meant for living with junk. Somewhere, in the midst of all that junk, is a very hungry, very naked man who possesses nothing.

My eight-year-old cousin knows what red corpuscles are and he could pilot a space ship to the moon, but he can't construct a graceful English sentence. He is inarticulate in the extreme and I attribute that to the fact that he is unreflective in the extreme. The teen-agers I teach could take my car apart nut by bolt by flywheel and put it back together again, but if I let them use the car they would drive to the most boring places imaginable. We have all learned too much and appropriated nothing. We have learned the secret of passing information from our senses directly into the convoluted, electrically connected, intellectually neuter pouches of our brains; and we have lost our minds.

"Fast food, fast cars and fast data delivery," that's what they'll write on our generation's headstone, if there is anyone left by then who can write. Real knowledge is a challenge, it teases the mind and stretches it to its limits. "Medium Cool" insinuates itself into brain cells; sleep-learning and mental programming are the ideal: they make no pretense at challenge, no attempts at wisdom — they deliver the data, the data that someone claims I need. When our culture finishes clouding half our minds with cheap emotion, it manipulates the other half into dullness by overstuffing it. The overall effect is to make us tired, to give us the sensation of satisfaction, to make us want to stop "knowing."

The human brain is an exquisite instrument. In a very concrete sense it is our link with reality. It functions to evaluate our sense experiences, to strain out the irrelevant, to store the essential and recall it when needed. If we train the brain to manage trivia we will kill it, and we will drive ourselves mad. The madness we will be driven to is the classical kind of madness: the madness of being separated from reality by a mental wall. Our culture's "data managers" and "data deliverers" in the advertising world, in the media, tell us what is real, what is essential; they rob us of our sanity by setting themselves up as a wall between us and reality. They replace the reality God created with a packaged version of the world, a package which can be measured and weighed but not savored, or loved, or saved. It is a sterile and colorless kind of psychosis they are packaging: it separates us from reality by wrapping us in sterile, brand name gauze. A man who is completely insulated from what is darkest in himself, and in the world around him, is also cut off from what is brightest. A man trapped in the safe middle range of his own potential is protected from his worst possibilities and isolated from his best.

Once again, our culture has accomplished its task of alienation not by downgrading the intellect, but by redefining it and by deifying the product of its own publicity. My brain is not the same as my intellect, and as a human being, a child of God, I long to have my intellect free again. I long for the freedom to know what God made and Who God is, not just to burrow deeper and deeper into my examination of the world other men have made for themselves.

The Christian is called upon to stand in witness against what the modern world has done by trivializing man's intellect. We have the mission of reaching the perfection of what we are called to be by our Father, and to make the Church more perfectly "the Body of Christ" by perfecting ourselves, the building blocks of that Body.

4. *Alienation from the World of the Spirit:*

Finally, our modern world has become alienated from the world of spiritual reality. It has accomplished this by a two-pronged attack on the spirit. On the one hand, there is a negative reaction to spirituality in our society which ranges from cynical dismissal to an outright attack on the viability of religious living in the modern world. On the other hand, there is a more subtle challenge: there is a popularization and a trivialization of religion in appeals to spiritism, the occult, demonology and "the Jesus trip." Religious experience is being cast in language calculated to compete with corn flakes commercials. I suspect that if our culture tries hard enough, it will be able to do to religious experience what it has already done to interpersonal relations: turn experience into sensation, expressive language into jargon, and the sincere urge to communicate into a madness to sell. The "spirit world" with which man must be in contact is not the mysterious world of "forces out there," it is the world of spirit within himself. A man must be able to sense deep within himself that which has been created "in the image and likeness of God." He must be able to sense within himself and within his community, the Church, the presence of the Holy Spirit of God.

* * * * *

In countless ways, then, our culture is alienating us from that which is deepest within us. It is trivializing our greatest gifts and glorifying all that is insignificant in order to create felt needs for what it can provide of its own creation. "Nothing begets nothing," and our culture has learned to package it most attractively. And we have learned to consume it passionately. Item number one on the agenda of a person who desires to be more prayerful must be the rediscovery of a culture which emphasizes man's integrity as a child of God. I can distort my own integrity by emphasizing the physical side of my nature; if I do so, I can achieve the sensation of prayer by the use of drugs. I can distort my own integrity by emphasizing the emotional side of my nature; if I do so, I can achieve the sensation of prayer by disconnecting myself from tradition, from rational reflection, and from the demands of living in a community larger than those I see face to face; by my intimate involvement in the world I can see and feel, I can dupe myself into believing I am in personal contact with God while, in fact, I am contacting nothing more than my own imagination. I can distort my own integrity by emphasizing the intellectual side of my nature; if I do so, I can achieve the sensation of prayer by orderly exercises, by deep reading, and by profound conversation. But in doing that, I will cut myself off from most of my being and from the vitality of the human community in which I live. In achieving that isolation, I will also isolate myself from the living and present truth of God's life among us today. Finally, I can also distort my own integrity by emphasizing the spiritual side of my nature; if I do so, I can achieve the sensation of prayer by my retreat into myself and away from the world around me; I can deny all that I experience outside of myself in favor of what I imagine I can experience inside of myself; I can begin to equate "spirit" with "psyche," and "prayer" with a kind of meditational "tripping."

In any case, I will have achieved a distortion, a disfigurement of the delicate balance the Lord has built into my being. By reconstructing my own nature and my own integrity I will have obscured God's image in myself. The method of prayer which I am about to outline draws on centuries of the Roman Catholic tradition of contemplative prayer. The method has its roots in the biblical vision of man as an integrated composite of body-feelings-mind-and-spirit. It borrows much from St. Benedict's ideal of "man the worshipper": a man who works with his hands, prays with voice and heart, and trains his mind to see God in the world He created. I offer this method as one which has brought me more spiritual growth than I ever imagined I could know, one which has made me hunger for more life still. I offer it with the prayer that it may lead you, too, to a deeper life with the Lord.

Part Two:
A Method Of
Contemplative Prayer
For Small Groups

CONTEMPLATIVE PRAYER

The word "contemplative" raises formidable images in some people's minds. It seems to some that only the austere solitude and silence of monastic living can generate real contemplation. It seems also that real contemplation can come only to those who have renounced the world entirely, and have taken up a posture of positive witness against the ways of secular culture by removing themselves from it.

Actually, this is a reversal of the truth: contemplative prayer does not *flow from* the decision to renounce the world, it *leads to* that disposition. The person who has committed himself to prayer is a person who is heading in the direction of making a renunciation of the world in some way. For some, that renunciation may be the total self-gift of monasticism; for most of us, our prayer moves us to live in the world while trying not to belong to it. The method of prayer I am about to outline is a method of contemplative prayer. It deserves that name for two reasons: first, it represents a way of renouncing the cultural values of the modern world for a man or woman who has already decided that the radical commitment of the monastic life is not a proper vocation for himself or herself; second, it witnesses against contemporary culture by attempting to reintegrate those four basic elements of man's life: the physical, the emotional, the intellectual, and the spiritual and it attempts to express that integration by "socialization" — by leading us to share the fruits of our prayer with other believers.

There are four basic steps to this method, parallelling the four areas of man's life which this method attempts to revitalize. These are followed by a fifth step whose aim is to help integrate the first four by sharing them with the Church. The method is centered on a passage from Scripture, or one of the ancient Fathers of the Church, or even on a selection from a more modern spiritual writer. The steps are:

(1) Reading aloud of the passage

(2) A "silent" reading of the passage in which the most important elements of the reading are turned over in the heart

(3) Meditation, in which the implications of the reading are analyzed in the mind

(4) Contemplation, or prayer itself, in which the one praying senses the presence of God

(5) Shared prayer, or the opportunity to bring what we have experienced in our private prayer to the attention of other believers for our mutual growth and enrichment.

After a few more general remarks about the method, I would like to offer a short, but more precise, description of each step and then offer you some "model prayers" or examples of the possible applications of this method.

WORD-CENTERED PRAYER

The method of prayer I am describing is "Word-centered" in several different senses. First of all, from the point of view of methodology, it is rooted in the words of a particular text from Scripture or some spiritual author. In other words, because we depend on a particular reading to begin the process of prayer, we can say that the process itself is dependent on words. But a clear distinction is necessary here: when I say that the method is "Word-centered," with a capital "W," I do not mean the words of the text — any text, including Scripture. When I use the expression "Word of God," I certainly don't mean the words of the Bible. I don't mean the English translation with which I deal, a translation constructed by the diligence and artifice of men. Nor do I mean the "originals" (or such manuscripts of them as have survived) from which the translations have been made, even though the originals would be the words the sacred authors were inspired by God to write. Rather, when I speak of the "Word of God," I mean the Word Himself, Jesus Christ, Who is the perfect expression of the Father's glory.

This then is a second sense in which this method is "Word-centered": not just that it begins with the words of a text, but that it proceeds to try to put me into contact with "*the* Word," Jesus. It is important to elaborate on this notion of "word" a bit more. In general, a word is a sign I try to make in order to reveal something which is hidden within me. Now there are many insignificant things hidden inside me, and the process by which I draw out words to express those things is, in itself, rather insignificant. Somewhere outside of me someone is asking, "Would you like a cup of tea?" Somewhere inside of me, hidden from everyone's view, I have a feeling that I don't want tea. Without great effort, and without any cost to myself beyond the expenditure of air and the vibration of my vocal chords, I say, "No, thank you, I don't care for tea just now."

But there are also some very significant things hidden inside of me. Somewhere outside of me a person for whom I care very deeply is moving. Somewhere deep inside me I sense my own feelings of love for the other. With great struggle, and with near terror, I take the risk of drawing out words to express my feelings. The process is immensely different from the one by which I express my preference for a certain drink; when I speak of love, what I am trying to do is to turn myself inside out. I would like to construct a word so powerful, so grand, so filled with beauty, so life-laden that it would contain my whole self (for, at this moment, it seems that my whole self is concentrated in the act of loving the other). But I am always the victim of my own humanity: the human model of speech is not as perfect as I would wish. There are no words so perfect and so lovely that they can bear a whole person. In fact, if I am to be honest about the matter, it's never my whole self that I want to communicate. At a given moment I may imagine that I am pouring my whole self into my love for another person, but a human being is a much more complicated creature than that. There are literally millions of parts to "me" and it's hard to think of any one act into which my whole self can be poured. There are simple sorts of conflicts, conflicts that can border on the humorous. A man can be anxious to give a terrific sales pitch to a prospective customer but, at the same time, he is ravenously hungry because he has skipped lunch; in the middle of his "pitch" his stomach growls and the customer laughs or, at least, is distracted. There are more complex and more touching conflicts, though. The man who is burning with love for another is also consumed with a fierce appetite for independence and self-reliance, and the two are in conflict. At one and the same time, he wants to hand himself over to another completely in love and to maintain his own freedom. We are quite complex, and outside of the most insignificant decisions of the day, we are torn by the complexity of our own needs and gifts.

Our words are often a hopeless tangle of revelation and obscurity. If I say that I love you, I am revealing the depths of my feelings for you but I am hiding the fact that I am jealous of my own independence. If I choose to speak only of my great desire for freedom and independence, I will reveal all of that to you but I will obscure the fact that my love is very deep. It is the complexity of human personality, in the speaker and in the hearer, that makes the "word" of human language such an ambiguous and limping bearer of meaning.

It is precisely the simplicity and unity of God's identity that makes His communication so perfect. God is not made of many parts: He is not sitting around wondering what to do with Himself in the next hour or so, facing all the conflicting pros and cons of acting this way or that. His freedom is not in conflict with His desire to give Himself in love. What He might be on the one hand is never in conflict with what He already is. It is His very essence to exist, to be what He is, to be God. It is His very essence to be perfect, to be without parts or divisions, to be One God. His desire to communicate is not, at first, a desire to communicate some insignificant sentiment or desire, it is a profound desire to share His whole self. Unlike us, His "self" is a unique and unitary thing, a perfect oneness, and His communication of Himself is His Word. In His Word, Jesus, He is able to do that which we are unable to do: He is able to put His whole self into that Word, to communicate all that He is in the Word, His Son, Jesus. As the ancient Fathers of the Church have pointed out, the only thing God the Father could not communicate to His Son was His own Fatherhood, and so His *Person* remains with Him — He remains Father, while Jesus remains Son — but, except for the relational identities of Their persons, They share all else in common because the Father has, from all time, communicated the full perfection of His unique and unitary being to the Son.

Let us stop here and summarize. There are two ways of communicating: the human way and the divine way. The human way of communicating is imperfect and tends to obscure as much as it reveals because we are such complex beings, creatures of so many different parts. Our words never really come up to our expectations for them; they never really accomplish the task of revealing us to one another. Divine communication, on the other hand, is perfect. God is able to become Word in Jesus. Jesus, begotten of the Father (not made by Him the way our words are "made" in our minds and our mouths), is the full and perfect revelation of all that the Father is. Among Themselves, the persons of the Trinity communicate life perfectly — They mutually offer and receive not only signs of Their identity, but the reality of that identity, and so They are *One God*.

How often, in moments of intimate communication, have we felt our identity to be in nearly perfect harmony with that of another person? And yet there is always the wall which stands between us, keeping us separate. In God the communication, the lack of selfishness, the complete self-possession are so perfect that the persons of the Trinity make complete gifts of Themselves to each other, and although there is no confusion of persons, each remaining uniquely Himself, Father, Son, and Spirit, there is an identity of being: together They are One God, the ground and source of all being.

What is most significant for us is the fact that God has freely decided not to limit His communication of Himself to the internal life of the Trinity. He has freely decided to offer Himself to man in revelation. We must recognize that there are two ways in which He has made this offer to us: first of all, borrowing our pedagogy, He has communicated with us through sign and symbol in word and action in history; second, however, He has also decided to communicate Himself to us by the personal gift He offers in the sacraments of the Church.

We must admit that there is a certain obscurity in His communication in so far as our pedagogy is concerned. In other words, because I am a complex creature, it is difficult for me to see through the words of the gospel to the Word which is Christ. The many thousands of people of His own day who heard Jesus did not understand the real meaning of His preaching and His signs. And finally, His own disciples, even Peter who professed his love three times, could not grasp the fullness of the message until they had been touched by the sacraments. But the Word of God has been transmitted to me in another way: in my Baptism that Word was planted in me by my being conformed to the death and resurrection of the Lord. In the Eucharist, it is brought to me again and again as the Word offers me the sign of His flesh and blood actually present in the sacrament. In all of the sacraments I am brought more and more deeply into contact with the Word, Jesus the Lord, Who by His initiative draws the whole Church into union with Himself through sacramental action.

In one sense, then, the Christian life requires study: it requires the hard work which will begin to clear away the obscurity that necessarily surrounds communication which is carried on in our human way. In His love for us, Jesus did communicate Himself to us in our way, and so real and honest prayer will always imply an interest in serious theology and a sincere attention to the Church's teaching authority. It is through these routes that we come, age by age, to understand the words and signs of Jesus more clearly. This is the very active phase of Christian living, the very active side of my prayer life. But there is also a more passive side, the part of me which longs quietly to plumb my own depths, to find the image of God within me, to make a deep act of faith in the sacraments I have received, to believe profoundly that the Word of God has taken up His dwelling within me, and that I can find Him if only I can be quiet and peaceful and serene enough.

It might be easy to say that the first of these two postures is the "apostolic" or "theological" project, while the second is the "contemplative." In fact, it is the integration of these two projects, the articulation that exists between them, that is the real essence of contemplation. The method of prayer I will outline is aimed at becoming *Word-centered*, at discovering the Word of God, Jesus, in the physical world, in my own feelings, in the truths my mind can uncover, in the life of the spirit which He has put within me, and within the Church and her history.

"*LECTIO APERTA*": READING ALOUD

In his autobiography, *The Seven Storey Mountain*, Thomas Merton describes his meeting with a certain Hindu monk known as Dr. Bramachari. At the time, individuals were asking Bramachari to suggest some mystical books, presuming that a Hindu monk would be in a position to suggest some esoteric oriental works which would help a Westerner break through to "real" spirituality. Bramachari suggested two books: St. Augustine's *Confessions* and *The Imitation of Christ*. I find that story relevant because of the way that our contemporaries, particularly young people, are in hot pursuit of the foreign and the esoteric in spirituality, never imagining that there might be any profundity in our own cultural tradition. Merton's observations about his meeting with Bramachari are worth remembering here:

> "He did not generally put his words in the form of advice: but the one counsel he did give me is something that I will not easily forget: 'There are many beautiful mystical books written by the Christians. You should read St. Augustine's *Confessions*, and *The Imitation of Christ*.'

> "Of course I had heard of both of them: but he was speaking as if he took it for granted that most people in America had no idea that such books ever existed" (Signet edition, p. 195).

Merton may be describing the world of the nineteen-thirties, but his words are quite applicable to the nineteen-seventies. If I speak of Hindu mantras I will arouse a great deal of interest in certain quarters, whereas if I point out that the Catholic tradition of contemplative prayer has always had an important place for repetition of vocal prayers no such interest will be forthcoming. But the fact, as Bramachari said, is that there is a great deal which is beautiful in our Christian tradition.

When I describe a method of prayer which begins with *lectio aperta*, or reading aloud, I am suggesting a value which is deeply ingrained in the Catholic tradition of repetitive vocal prayer as a route to contemplation, and also ingrained in the notion of the Hindu mantra. The mantra is a secret word, a word unique to the individual, a word which has power to evoke the personal identity of the user of the mantra. I would claim, in a parallel way, that there is a Word which has the power to release your identity as a Christian; there is a Word which, once you know and love it, can recreate you, liberate you from all that holds you back from being yourself, and bring all your greatest potentials to fulfillment. That Word is Jesus, and that Word is deep within you. Reading aloud is the beginning of the prayer because it sets up a rhythm of prayer, it sets up a cadence of peace and concentration. The word of the text is meant to evoke the Living Word within me. The same Holy Spirit Who inspired the author of a particular piece of Scripture, the Spirit Who filled the heart of some other spiritual writer is the same Spirit which has been given to me in my Baptism and my Confirmation, the same Spirit which is the Soul of the Church. As St. Paul says, "The Spirit too comes to help us in our weakness. For when we cannot choose words in order to pray properly, the Spirit himself expresses our plea in a way that could never be put into words, and God who knows everything in our hearts, knows perfectly well what he means, and that the pleas of the saints expressed by the Spirit are according to the word of God" (*Romans 8:26-27*).

A careful, slow, reverent, vocal reading of the text which will form the basis of my prayer is essential: it is essential to use the voice and breathing as aids to establishing the atmosphere for prayer, and to create a special respect for the words of the text itself. This careful reading is also an implied act of faith: that I believe that God wills that I should know Him and sense His presence by giving myself over to His word in Scripture and to the words of those whom He has tested and found worthy of Himself.

"LECTIO TACITA": SILENT READING

After I have composed myself and read the passage at hand aloud, carefully and reverently, I pause to collect my thoughts and feelings. The second step of the method is to repeat what I have read silently. Now I am not speaking about memorization of the whole text, or any part of it. The point of this second step is that, after a careful and faith-filled reading, some particular words or phrases in the text will strike me as being particularly moving. If the whole passage has been about sin and forgiveness, for example, there will have been some words about the depths of sin, or the richness of God's mercy, which will have moved me in a special way.

In the first phase, oral reading, I am trying to use my body, the physical gift of voice which God has given me to praise Him and to open my heart to Him. Here, in this second phase, I am trying to open my emotions and feelings to Him. I am trying to locate the elements within the passage which have had the most appeal to my own sentiments. I think of the way the great mystics allowed themselves to be consumed by their own feelings of sorrow and horror over the Passion of our Lord, and use that profound feeling as a first step to the deep union of prayer. In the same way we are trying, in this second phase, to open our feelings to the power and presence of God.

"MEDITATIO": MEDITATION

Next, we are attempting to draw our intellect into the new "cultural integration" of prayer by finding meanings and generalizations within a given reading. Again, extending the example of a reading which would concern itself with sin and forgiveness, having read the story aloud and having explored the feelings which it arouses in me, I can train my mind to analyze the implications of the story. I can draw from it generalized lessons about sin and about the merciful forgiveness of God.

I recall that St. Thomas Aquinas said that the formal object of theology was not knowledge but love. Because man is a complex creature, because he has a mind and an insatiable hunger for knowledge, he does pursue God, seeking to understand His life and gifts. But the purpose of our pursuit is to love Him and share His life with Him, not to obtain abstract information to share with each other at ecclesiastical cocktail parties and prayer meetings.

"CONTEMPLATIO/ORATIO": CONTEMPLATION/PRAYER

This step, of course, is the hardest to describe since it is the heart of the method I am proposing here. To put it briefly, the contemplation I am suggesting is not man's attempt to contemplate God but man's realization that God is contemplating him. In the Catholic tradition we have always maintained the distinction between "active" and "passive" contemplation: "active" contemplation being man's efforts to penetrate somewhat into the mystery of the Trinity's life, "passive" contemplation being man's surrender of himself to the Trinity's efforts to penetrate sacramentally and mystically into man's life.

That mystical interpenetration of God and the praying soul cannot be programmed into any method of prayer. At the very least, I can encourage you to be "active," to seek out a deeper sense of the mystery of God's presence. But I can also encourage you to be faithful to this method, to be patient in waiting for the Lord and in believing that He does come. Again, continuing with the example of a reading about sin and forgiveness, the perfection of prayer would be to have this experience: that while I am using my voice to emphasize my physical devotion to God, and while I am searching my emotions for my deepest feelings about sin and God's mercy, and while I am using my mental powers to analyze and derive deeper meaning from what I have read, while all of this is going on, I am suddenly taken hold of by the awareness that *at this very moment while I am struggling to find God in things physical, emotional, and intellectual, He has already found me in the innermost core of my being.* While I recite, and mull over, and reflect on the theme of forgiveness, He is loving and forgiving me. While I search for Him, He has found me. This is real prayer: to be caught up by the Lord Who has already found you. I pray, first and foremost, for this gift of prayer.

"COLLATIO": SHARED PRAYER

Priests who were in the seminary twenty years ago, and religious Brothers and Sisters who were in formation at about the same time, will remember the institution of the *collatio* in the middle of the morning or the afternoon. It simply meant a light snack which was permitted at some point during the day; it usually consisted of a cup of chocolate and a few biscuits eaten together in the common dining room.

The history of the word and the notion is quite interesting. In fact, *collatio* was originally the last step of the monk's daily voyage in prayer. Having prayed aloud and silently, "with loud cries and silent tears," having searched for the Lord and having been found by Him, the monk came together with his brothers to share his experiences, to thank God for the gift of prayer and, perhaps, to ask for the same gifts for a brother who was experiencing difficulty. As the centuries passed the fellowship remained, supplemented by a warm drink, but the depth of spiritual sharing was lost.

In fact, in our own day, when I hear the expression "shared prayer" I usually shudder because I know how often it means a substitute for prayer. I've talked elsewhere about the hollowness and vacuity of shared prayer which replaces the hard work of private prayer. This *collatio* is to be the last step, the urge of charity, that flows from my private prayer.

THE SHARING GROUP

Forming a group for sharing this kind of prayer is not an easy matter. It is not simply an organizational task. I remember listening to a preacher years ago who offered a very humorous rewriting of St. Peter's speech on Pentecost Sunday: "You Parthians, Medes, and Elamites will meet on Thursdays at 8 o'clock, in the Church basement. Inhabitants of Mesopotamia, Judaea and Cappadocia can come on Tuesday mornings at 10 or on Wednesday evenings at 8" (*cf. Acts 2:9ff.*).

If you are really interested in forming a group with whom you can share prayer in this way, then I suggest that you invite some of your friends to read through this method, to study the model prayers at the end of the book and then try it. People will have to find one another naturally in this. There will have to be a discovery of a natural desire to pray aided by God's supernatural motivation and grace, all bound together by an inclination to follow this particular method. If all of that comes together correctly, you will have a group which can offer mutual support, encouragement, and love to one another as each member struggles to grow in the Lord.

Part Three:
Model Prayers

Model Prayers

The method of prayer which I have described in the preceding section can really be applied to any text which you may find moving. However, at the outset, it is best to apply the method to classical religious texts, texts which suggest clear guidelines for religious reflection. Texts from Scripture are obviously suitable for this use but texts from the ancient Fathers of the Church may also be found to be rich sources for reflection. It is interesting to note that although patristic texts have a certain "sacredness" about them as far as we are concerned, primitive monks who used them as sources for prayer would have thought of them with less awe than we ourselves. Nevertheless, it is worthwhile to begin with these nearly universally admired writings before proceeding to more modern texts.

I have tried to construct these prayers carefully so as to demonstrate the way in which the richness of classical and patristic texts can be brought to bear on modern works, emphasizing the continuity of religious reflection throughout the history of God's revelation of Himself to man. At the beginning, I will provide Scriptural and classical patristic texts for your consideration and prayer.

My purpose in this final section is to help you to become accustomed to the application of the method of prayer I have outlined, and to show some of the potential riches of this method. I will be describing some "model prayers" based on a few common Scriptural passages and on some patristic texts with which you may not be familiar. My ultimate purpose is to encourage you to select other passages of your own and to use them to begin praying more deeply.

Before proceeding to the models, it may be helpful to provide a summary outline of the method I have described.

1. *Lectio Aperta*, "reading aloud":

Choose a text which will provide the starting point for your prayer; spend a few moments relaxing before approaching the text; try to shut out distracting thoughts, especially worrisome ones; read the text aloud, as slowly as is practical and meaningful; try to catch the rhythm of the words; use your voice and your breathing to help create a mood, and to create a detachment from everything but the text at hand; remember that the reading aloud is akin to the oriental mantra, or the Jesus prayer, in which one is carried along by the power of certain words.

2. *Lectio Tacita*, "quiet reading":

Quietly repeat to yourself the words or phrases in the text which have moved you most; concentrate on the feelings that these words and phrases have evoked in you; you are not trying to locate great meaning, or to rehash the ideas of the text in an intellectual way; the purpose is to recapture some special, loving moment you experienced in reading the original text.

3. *Meditatio*, "meditation":

Think of the implications of your feelings about the text; examine your feelings to discover what you can learn about God and about yourself from what you have felt about the text; try to connect what you have read and your own feelings about what you have read with what you already know about God and His way of dealing with you; in reading aloud, use your voice and breathing to alert yourself to the presence of God; in quiet reading use your feelings for the same purpose; now in the meditation you are to allow your mind and your intellect to be channels of God's gracious self-gift.

4. *Contemplatio*, or *Oratio*, "contemplation":

This is the real prayer, the moment in which we try to sense the presence of God deep within ourselves; not my intellectual and emotional struggle to contemplate God, but my personal surrender to the fact that God is contemplating me; even as I am struggling to locate my feelings and to prod my mind into activity so that I can find God, He has already taken hold of me, and is engaged in the deepest possible understanding of my identity and my whole being; in the following models, this stage can only be suggested for each prayer.

5. *Collatio*, "shared prayer":

Go to meet with others who have prayed alone in their lives and seek and offer mutual support by sharing your feelings, understanding, and experience of the Lord as you have known Him in your prayer; this sharing also helps to test your prayer: to test it against the *whole* community's experience of the Lord; this sharing is not to be the quasi-psychological device of announcing my darkest secrets out loud in front of others in order to gain sympathy and friendship and consolation — it is to be the *report* that I *have found* consolation with the Lord because I have laid all my burdens on Him; since our "models" deal only with the private part of the prayer, and cannot suggest how the shared experience will proceed, you are simply encouraged throughout to seek the presence of others who will be willing to undertake this method of prayer with you.

"Zacchaeus, Come Down!"

1. *Reading aloud:*

"*Jesus entered Jericho and was going through the town when a man whose name was Zacchaeus made his appearance; he was one of the senior tax collectors and a wealthy man. He was anxious to see what kind of man Jesus was, but he was too short and could not see him for the crowd; so he ran ahead and climbed a sycamore tree to catch a glimpse of Jesus who was to pass that way. When Jesus reached the spot he looked up and spoke to him: 'Zacchaeus, come down. Hurry, because I must stay at your house today.' And he hurried down and welcomed him joyfully. They all complained when they saw what was happening. 'He has gone to stay at a sinner's house' they said. But Zacchaeus stood his ground and said to the Lord, 'Look, sir, I am going to*

*give half my property to the poor, and if I have
cheated anybody I will pay him back four times the
amount.' And Jesus said to him, 'Today salvation has
come to this house, because this man too is a son of
Abraham; for the Son of Man has come to seek out
and save what was lost'* " *(Luke 19:1-10).*

2. *Quiet reading:*

Repeat some of the passages which have inspired
strong feelings in you. For example:

" *. . . he was anxious to see what kind of man Jesus
was*"

Like Zacchaeus, I am hungry to know Who Jesus
is and what He is like. I want to see Him face to face,
from a new point of view. I have heard of other
people who have said remarkable things about Jesus,
I have heard that He has done wonderful and powerful things in their lives, brought them the peace and
the security which I want so very much. I want to
know if He really has that power, I want to know if
He can bring to me the same healing power others
say He has brought to them.

" *. . . he was too short and could not see him*"

I have so many deficiencies in my life. Zacchaeus'
own size and the pressing crowd around him cut off
his view of Jesus. In a very similar way, the combina-
tion of my personal weaknesses and the pressures of
the world around me make it so very difficult for me
to see and understand Christ's identity and His power. As much as I may hunger for knowledge of Him
and for a share of His life I am so often frustrated at
my own inability to pray and sense His presence.

" . . . he ran ahead and climbed a sycamore tree to catch a glimpse of Jesus"

Zacchaeus faced his problem and acted imaginatively to correct it, and so must I. Prayer is the "sycamore tree" for me, it is the new point of view, the "high place" to which I must rise in order to see Jesus. In my prayer I am attempting to gain a new perspective, to use all that is human in me including my senses and my mind, to uncover and liberate what is "divine" in me: the image of God buried deep within me, and the gentle urgings of His Holy Spirit live in me because of my baptism and my membership in the Church.

" . . . Jesus . . . was to pass that way"

If my mind and heart can be truly serene and really open, I will see that Jesus is always "passing" through my life. Zacchaeus may have seen Jesus' presence in Jericho that day as a fortunate accident, but from Jesus' point of view that encounter was destined from all eternity. It is no accident that Christ is inviting me to know Him and feel His presence on a given occasion. From all time He has planned to make the *total* gift of Himself to me at *all* times. He is offering me the chance to know Him, to feel His presence, and to share His life and love with others each and every day of my life.

" . . . I must stay at your house today"

While I go through the contortions of my attempts to lay hold of Christ, while I climb sycamore trees and bend over backwards in my attempts to see Him, He is looking for me and He is filled with desire to be with me. While I am struggling to find a way to

111

be with Him, imagining that I must find some "secret route" to heaven in order to find Him, He is at my door, at every possible "opening" of my soul, inviting Himself in to *my* home, to my world, and to my life. As He once took the radical step of sharing our flesh, so He is still taking radical initiatives to be with us in our world and our lives.

" . . . They all complained when they saw what was happening"

I am so afraid of how men will react if they know I am struggling to pray. I imagine they will see through me, find out my secret, and know how profoundly unworthy I am of Christ's interest. My own fear often keeps me from praying, and drives me to think that I should try to improve myself morally and humanly before approaching Christ. I will have to learn with Zacchaeus that the Lord has a way of moving into my life, of turning all of my values upside down, and of pointing out what is really important to Him and to me.

" . . . this man too is a son of Abraham"

Zacchaeus thought his generosity and his conversion to honesty would bring him salvation, but Jesus looked deep into the man's soul, far beyond the signs and symbols Zacchaeus was trying to drag out of himself. Salvation did come to him, but it was not salvation on his own terms, salvation at the price he imagined: it was salvation as the pure gift of God, it was salvation that was rooted in Zacchaeus' identity, not in his actions. And, what is most important, that identity was itself God's gift. I am a son of Abraham in faith; I am a son of the Church; I too am a child of

God. Christ peers deeply into my soul and sees the secret of my identity, the secret of the baptismal power that has changed me once and for all into a new creation. Salvation will come to me when I am liberated from my own strivings and become open to God's free gift, to His loving acceptance of the good work He has begun in me and sustains with His power.

3. *Meditation:*

Jesus is picking me out of the world each day, He is electing me from the crowd and He is seeking me out to be with me. The saving power He is offering is not a reward for my virtues, it is a refreshment for the soul that comes when I recognize His efforts to seek me out. God is constantly expressing His unique identity by offering His presence and love. It is His very nature to attempt to be with me — not in bits and pieces, not in mysteries and magic, but in His entirety each day. It is my task in prayer to make the effort to open my mind and heart to His will to be with me. My prayer is not a process of searching obscure books for some strange and personal meanings, it is not a process of developing increasing sensitivity to what I may imagine is God's "special interventions" in the daily routines of my life. It is a process of sharpening my sensitivity to the fact that the life and death and resurrection of Jesus have been the most "special" kind of intervention conceivable. At all times *God is being Himself*, and it is His nature to reveal Himself and share Himself with me through His Word, just as surely as it is my nature to be open to Him and to His total self-gift.

4. Contemplation:

At this point I wait quietly and patiently for the Lord to move. I hope for His Holy Spirit to take hold of me. I want to be "caught unawares" and to be seized by the deep recognition that while I am struggling to understand and feel the way in which He offered Himself to Zacchaeus, He will open my heart to see that He is making the same offer to me, now.

* * * * *

"Lord, You sought Zacchaeus out of the crowd and found him while he was looking for You. You are here, with me and within me. I have opened my senses, I have converted my feelings, I have exercised my mind, all for You. Now, let all restraints fall away from me, free me from my struggle and frustration, give me healing power through Your Holy Spirit. Give me silence and Your gift of prayer. Let all words and thoughts and feelings cease and be consumed in Your loving presence. For this moment, let me dissolve in wonder at Your presence. Look through me, as You looked through Zacchaeus, look deeply through me to the core of my being and see there the son You have adopted, see there Jesus Who is Your true and only Son, and give me the gift of Your vision to see myself as You do."

"Seek The Lord, That You May Live"

The following selection is from the writings of Gregory of Narek, an Armenian priest, poet, and mystic who lived from 944 to 1010. This particular passage is the twelfth prayer in Gregory's *The Book of Prayers.*

1. *Reading aloud:*

   " 'Everyone who calls on the name of the Lord will be saved.'

   "As for myself, not only do I invoke him, but above all I believe in his greatness.

   "It is not for his gifts
   that I persevere in my supplications,
   but because he is true Life
   and the true cause of respiration,

without whom there is neither movement nor
   progress.

"Indeed, it is not so much by the bond of hope
   as by the ties of love that I am attracted.
   It is not the gifts but the Giver for whom I continually pine.

"It is not glory for which I aspire,
   but it is the Glorified One that I seek to embrace.
   It is not by the desire for life
   but by the memory of the One who gives life
   that I am ever consumed!
   It is not after the passion for pleasures that I
   strive,
   but it is out of the desire for the One who pre-
   pares them
   that from the depths of my heart I burst into
   tears.

"It is not repose that I seek,
   but the visage of the One who gives repose
   that I suppliantly request.

"It is not for the nuptial banquet
   but out of desire for the Bridegroom that I lan-
   guish.

"In the certain expectation of his power
   despite the burden of my transgressions
   I believe with unwavering hope,
   entrusting myself in the hand of the Almighty,
   that not only will I obtain pardon
   but I will also see him in person,
   thanks to his mercy and pity,
   thus inheriting heaven for myself
   although I fully deserve to be deprived of it."

2. *Quiet reading:*

Repeat some of the passages which have inspired strong feelings in you. For example:

"*. . . not only do I invoke him . . . I believe in his greatness*"

The vitality of my prayer is not in the energy I invest in praying. The real life of it is in the depth of my fundamental believing in God. Behind my efforts at prayer, behind my style of religious living, far behind all that there is about my faith there must be solid rock. And that rock is this: that deep in my own inmost being I know that the Lord lives. I sense my own life, my own destiny to live forever, and in that sensation I find the Lord Who has given me life. Far more than my prayer, it is the grace to believe which He has given to me which is the rock-bottom foundation of my growth in His life.

"*. . . he is true life and the true cause of respiration*"

How often I confuse my living with my life. How easily I imagine that I can understand myself by examining the frothy waves I stir up around myself as I move through the world. How captivated I am by the project of pretending to see myself when I am only looking at what I have produced in others. Even my common-sense language gives away my real hope: I speak of *my* body, *my* mind, *my* life, and in every common-sense word I am affirming my secret belief that I am more than all these things, that there is an identity beyond and beneath them all that is *me*. The Lord is my true life, He is the only One in Whom I can find my true self. The secret of my life is the secret He knew when He created me from nothing.

" . . . it is not the gifts but the Giver for whom I continually pine"

So often I have set goals for myself, goals in everyday living and goals of spiritual growth. When I seem to have achieved them I am as hungry as I was before. Or, what is worse, I am more terrified for having achieved them because I fear that they will not last. It seems to be the activity and growth and faith and prayer that I want, but it is not true. What I want is the One to Whom my activity is directed, the One toward Whom I am growing, the One in Whom I have placed my faith, the One to Whom I am praying. Some fear holds me back from admitting it, but the truth is this: nothing short of God Himself can possibly satisfy all my longings.

" . . . it is not by the desire for life but by the memory of the One who gives life that I am ever consumed!"

How can it be that I long for the Lord? How can it be that I am consumed and driven by deep desire to move towards something and someone I do not really know? God, the source of my life, is at the back of my mind, and on the horizon of my vision, like a memory I cannot quite call up, like something or someone I once knew, but have not seen face to face in a long time. All of my religious activity is drawing up bits and pieces of that memory from the deepest, most personal place within myself. All of it strives for one thing only: that I may find myself swallowed up in the life of the One Who gave me life.

" . . . it is not repose that I seek, but the visage of the One who gives repose"

As I strive to grow in faith and in prayer I imagine that what I want is rest, security, a real spiritual life; but it is all quite false. What I want is not the rest and quiet, not the cessation of all my activities, but their fulfillment. My real goal is the One Who is hidden in the image of rest that is lodged in my mind, the One Who is enfolded in my vision of absence of struggle and contradiction and frustration and disappointment. I know that once I have found Him I will never really rest again, I will never again know the emptiness of inactivity. Once I know Him as He knows me I will be full of a new, and more peace-bearing energy, an energy I will never consume in my peace at being with Him.

3. Meditation:

The Lord is calling me to be with Him, to find my rest and the fulfillment of my life in Him. From the day of my baptism, and through each day of the Church's witness to the death and resurrection of Christ, I have been receiving that call. Often I have heard it, more often I have been deafened by the noise of the world about me and the world within me. I really should not busy myself with the hundreds of details of the spiritual life, as if I could manage to get any satisfying peace from them, as if I could "add one cubit" to my spiritual stature by them. My vision must be fixed on the One Who has power to give me life and growth, it must be fixed on Father and Son and Spirit, on God Himself. All that I do and experience in faith is simply a collection of ways that I prepare myself for the meeting with the Lord. It is in prayer — not my style of prayer, but His gift of prayer, and in sacraments that I will meet Him here in this world. Finally, it is beyond death that I will know Him as I am known by Him. All of my faith is only a temporary moment, for it will all pass when I will know Him with my whole self, not only in faith. All of my hope will vanish, when what I hope for is mine by God's gracious self-gift. It is only my love for Him which will endure, and its endurance is promised by His eternal love for me.

4. Contemplation:

"Come, Lord Jesus! Let all of my unsubstantial visions of the things around me dissolve. Burst forth, through them, to show Yourself as the true object of all my longing and all my living. Come, find me as I search for You. Come bathe me in Your light and save me from fanning the flame of my own burning, raging darkness. Let me love my life in this world so deeply that the love of it will break my heart with joy and expectation of Your life, the true life that gives life to all."

"To Have What Must Die Taken Up Into Life"

1. *Reading aloud:*

"*For we know that when the tent that we live in on earth is folded up, there is a house built by God for us, an everlasting home not made by human hands, in the heavens. In this present state, it is true, we groan as we wait with longing to put on our heavenly home over the other; we should like to be found wearing clothes and not without them. Yes, we groan and find it a burden being still in this tent, not that we want to strip if off, but to put the second garment over it and to have what must die taken up into life. This is the purpose for which God made us, and he has given us the pledge of the Spirit*" (2 Corinthians 5:1-5).

2. *Quiet reading:*

Repeat some of the passages which have inspired strong feelings in you. For example:

"*. . . the tent that we live in on earth*"

How fragile is my life in this world. What startling fragility there is in my dependence on things for my body's survival; what a terrible power nature has over me, that it can snuff out my life, "fold up my tent" in a moment! But there is more to my life than my body, and there is more to my fragile state than my physical dependences. The whole fabric of my living is a delicate, woven thing. The fibers of so many lives, and so many joys and sufferings have been plaited together through the years of my living. Patient hands have fashioned it; the loving hands of my parents and teachers and friends; the selfish hands of those who have sought to use me; the pleading hands of those I have used without love. But the work of these human hands is fragile, too; it too will fold one day.

"*. . . an everlasting home not made by human hands, in the heavens*"

By all that He has said and done Jesus has called me to another home. He has not called me to life in a fragile tent, but to life that is without end. He has called me to live in the image and likeness of His Father, Who is in heaven. The source of all life is calling me to live, to live forever with Him. "The sadness of death gives way to the bright promise of immortality!" (*From the Roman Liturgy*).

"*. . . to put on our heavenly home over the other*"

For all its fragility I love the "tent" that has been

fashioned for me. I forget none of my earthly joys, and I regret none of my sorrows: all of them have been gifts of God woven by human hands into the fabric of my life. Though I long for the new life, the full life of His kingdom, I do not long to destroy my body and its life. I do not wish to obliterate what I have done and what has been done to me while I have lived in this tent. I believe firmly in Christ's power to redeem all things. I believe firmly in His anxiousness to take all of my life to Himself, and to transform it, bit by bit and moment by moment, into the pure spiritual fabric of a new life which will be forever. This "tent" is already the beginning of my fullness of life with Him.

" . . . to have what must die taken up into life"

The mark and the pain of death is on all of my living. The man who lives in misery longs for death as release. The man who loves living fears death because of its power to corrupt joy and destroy earthly pleasure. The man of the Spirit is caught between longing for and fearing death, but he knows that there is a mystery: death does not end life, it only advances it one great step. In His power, Christ will finally draw *all* things to Himself, and even the most fragile of mortal things will be swallowed up in His life. There is no oblivion in the Christian's death, there is only new and deeper awareness, full self-possession because I will be fully possessed by the Lord. There is a resolution of all conflicts and a fulfillment of all hopes. There is a new and heightened awareness of all that I have done, an awareness that participates in God's ability to love me in all that I have done and known and loved and feared.

" . . . the pledge of the Spirit"

His Holy Spirit is with me in the world, in my life. His presence is the continuing pledge that my life is moving towards resolution and wholeness. In every suffering and in every joy there is an opening toward immortality. In every moment there is a door that leads to eternity. As moments pass, as they perish and tumble upon one another, the Spirit of Jesus is with me pointing the way to my true destiny. In His power I live and breathe, in His promise I have placed all my hope, in His presence I have no fear.

3. *Meditation:*

Our life in the world is not a test to which we are condemned to determine our worthiness for the "other" life. There is only *one* life, the life of God. He shares that life with us in the measure in which we can bear it. I do not long for death because I have no desire to see the end of what He has created for me. My longing is to see the fullness of life which is only hinted at in my living, it is to taste the perfection of love which I sample here as I give and receive in my loving other men. I believe deeply that I will live forever, and that my body will rise from the dust. I know that the Lord will raise my body to life again as the final seal of all the goodness of earthly living as He created it. I long for the day when all that is mortal will be dissolved in immortality.

4. *Contemplation:*

"Lord Jesus, send Your Holy Spirit to me to lead me gently to see the beauty of the world You have created. Soften my heart to love creation more deeply. This world is not a prison; it is the same world which held Your body and nourished You and gave You breath. You, Who are God and man, lead me above all to love my own body and to respect and cherish it. Let me enjoy it fully and reasonably so that I may bring it to You on the last day marked with all of its joys and sorrows but free of any mark of selfishness or disrespect. Come take what is mortal in me and draw it up into Your life. Open my eyes and my heart to see the signs of eternal life in the moments of earthly life which You have allotted for my growth."

About The Author

Father Alan Placa was born in New York City. After working in politics, studying medicine and teaching science, he finally turned to the Church and was ordained a priest of the Diocese of Rockville Centre in 1970. He has served as Assistant Pastor in a suburban parish where he formed an Adult School of Theology. He is currently Dean of Students at St. Pius X Seminary. Father Placa is a well-known and popular lecturer in the New York area and has published several articles on spiritual and sacramental subjects.

Books by Venard Polusney, O. Carm.

UNION WITH THE LORD IN PRAYER
Beyond Meditation To Affective Prayer Aspiration And Contemplation
.85

"A magnificent piece of work. It touches on all the essential points of Contemplative Prayer. Yet it brings such a sublime subject down to the level of comprehension of the 'man in the street,' and in such an encouraging way."
Abbott James Fox, O.C.S.O. (former superior of Thomas Merton at the Abbey of Gethsemani)

ATTAINING SPIRITUAL MATURITY FOR CONTEM-PLATION (According to St. John of the Cross)
.85

"I heartily recommend this work with great joy that at last the sublime teachings of St. John of the Cross have been brought down to the understanding of the ordinary Christian without at the same time watering them down. For all (particularly for charismatic Christians) hungry for greater contemplation."
Rev. George A Maloney, S.J., Editor of Diakonia, Professor of Patristics and Spirituality, Fordham University.

THE PRAYER OF LOVE . . . THE ART OF ASPIRATION
1.50

"It is the best book I have read which evokes the simple and loving response to remain in love with the Lover. To read it meditatively, to imbibe its message of love, is to have it touch your life and become part of what you are."
Mother Dorothy Guilbault, O. Carm., Superior General, Lacombe, La.

From the writings of John of St. Samson, O. Carm., mystic and charismatic

PRAYER, ASPIRATION AND CONTEMPLATION
Translated and edited by Venard Poslusney, O. Carm.   **Paper 3.95**

All who seek help in the exciting journey toward contemplation will find in these writings of John of St. Samson a compelling inspiration and support along with the practical guidance needed by those who travel the road of prayer.

CRISIS OF FAITH: Invitation to Christian Maturity   1.50

By Rev. Thomas Keating, ocso. How to hear ourselves called to discipleship in the Gospels is Abbot Thomas' important and engrossing message. As Our Lord forms His disciples, and deals with His friends or with those who come asking for help in the Gospels, we can receive insights into the way He is forming or dealing with us in our day to day lives.

DISCOVERING PATHWAYS TO PRAYER   1.75

By Msgr. David E. Rosage. Following Jesus was never meant to be dull, or worse, just duty-filled. Those who would aspire to a life of prayer and those who have already begun, will find this book amazingly thorough in its scripture-punctuated approach.

"A simple but profound book which explains the many ways and forms of prayer by which the person hungering for closer union with God may find him." **Emmanuel Spillane, O.C.S.O., Abbott, Our Lady of the Holy Trinity Abbey, Huntsville, Utah.**

SEEKING PURITY OF HEART:
THE GIFT OF OURSELVES TO GOD   illus 1.25

By Joseph Breault. For those of us who feel that we do not live up to God's calling, that we have sin of whatever shade within our hearts. This book shows how we can begin a journey which will lead from our personal darkness to wholeness in Christ's light — a purity of heart. Clear, practical help is given us in the constant struggle to free ourselves from the deceptions that sin has planted along all avenues of our lives.

ENFOLDED BY CHRIST: An Encouragement to Pray   1.95

By Rev. Michael Hollings. This book helps us toward giving our lives to God in prayer yet at the same time remaining totally available to our fellowman — a difficult but possible feat. Father's sharing of his own difficulties and his personal approach convince us that "if he can do it, we can." We find in the author a true spiritual guardian and friend.